Conservation and Preservation
of Humanities Research Collections

WASHINGTONIANA

WASH
REF
025.84
C754

Conservation and Preservation of Humanities Research Collections

Essays on Treatment and Care of Rare Books, Manuscripts, Photography, and Art on Paper and Canvas

Edited by Dave Oliphant
With an Introduction by James Stroud

Harry Ransom Humanities Research Center • The University of Texas at Austin

*Copyright© 1989 by the Harry Ransom Humanities Research Center,
The University of Texas at Austin*

ISBN 0-87959-109-9

Cover illustration: Burned fragment of a poem by William Faulkner. *HRHRC Collections*. Photographed by Patrick Keeley.

Contents

JAMES STROUD *Introduction*	7
KAREN PAVELKA *Conservation Treatment of a Bound Manuscript in the Byron Collection*	23
CAROL SUE WHITEHOUSE *D.H. Lawrence's "The First Lady Chatterley": Conservation Treatment of a Twentieth-Century Bound Manuscript*	41
ELLEN WEIR *Conservation of the Burned Fragments in the William Faulkner Collection*	57
JILL WHITTEN *A Summer Internship in Paintings Conservation*	79
MARY C. BAUGHMAN *Treatments of Five Nineteenth-Century Cloth Case-Bound Books*	87
SUE MURPHY *Conserving Art for Traveling Exhibition: Treatment of a Storyboard*	105
BRUCE LEVY *The "K-118" Binding Structure: A 500-Year-Old Experiment for Modern-Day Book Conservation*	117
BARBARA BROWN *Henry Peach Robinson's "Bringing Home the May": Conservation Treatment of a Nineteenth-Century Albumen Print*	135
FRANK YEZER *Housing, When and Why*	149
ELLEN CUNNINGHAM-KRUPPA *The General Libraries Preservation Program: A Preliminary Report*	157
Notes on Contributors	164
Index to "The Library Chronicle," New Series Numbers 42-45, 1988	167

Valerie Tresse (foreground), an intern from the University of Paris, Sorbonne, and Karen Pavelka, assistant paper conservator, perform treatments on manuscripts and art on paper.

Introduction

Had Harry Huntt Ransom not been the visionary he was when he founded in 1957 the Humanities Research Center of The University of Texas at Austin; had he elected to pursue the development of the Center's collections in the customary manner of the late 1950s by expending funds solely in the acquisition of works by Romantic and earlier writers deemed appropriate for the traditional university book and manuscript repository, the HRC would have had a reputable collection. Only modest amounts of conservation treatment might then have been necessary to ensure the long-term preservation of such holdings. Dr. Ransom's efforts were, however, more daring, and his acquisition of vast numbers of modern literary manuscripts, publishers' and newspapers' archives, private papers and correspondence, and photographic and iconographic images has resulted in an extraordinary and unique collection of twentieth-century archival and research materials. Along with this collection came the extraordinary problems of its care. Research centers whose focus is in pre- and early nineteenth-century collections face preservation challenges from many ravages associated with the passage of time, but none of these is so critical as the destructive effects on modern library holdings of the poor-quality materials from which such collections are made.

Modern developments in the production of materials used for the making of paper and books and the media employed in modern printing, writing, and artistic endeavors changed the course of preservation technology and conservation treatment. The quantity of paper required to satisfy a growing public demand necessitated the use of cheaper products and faster production systems; consequently, paper made prior to the nineteenth century has proven to be much more durable than paper manufactured more recently. The long-term ramifications of the chemical processes initially employed to produce a clean and attractive paper from chips of wood were slow in being completely understood at the paper mills whose management was simply more interested in meeting a rapidly increasing demand for such a product. The growth of the coal-tar dye industry opened a multitude of commercial opportunities for the pigment and ink manufacturers, and again, the pressures of supply and demand drove products into the marketplace too rapidly for any assessment of the long-term stability of the inks, watercolors, and artists' paints being produced. Because of their colorful and attractive appearance, such products gained wide popularity among the writers and artists responsible for our modern artistic and literary heritage. Similarly, the manufacturers of leather succumbed to economic necessity by increasing production rates at the cost of chemical stability and overall quality of the skins which were used to cover books and encase historical documents. A wide range of developments in the adhesives industry saw the production of numerous new products which made life for the binder, the artist, the author, and the craftsman easier. Pressure sensitive adhesive tapes and rubber-based contact adhesives permitted a much more rapid and flexible approach to revisions, paste-ups, and publishers' dummies for both the author and the publisher. Because of the temporary nature of such draft formats, the rapid deterioration of these adhesives was not viewed with much concern. Bookbinding, like other crafts and skills which became so mechanized that they barely resembled the sixteenth- and seventeenth-century practices from which they grew, suffered from the same pressures to institute assembly-line production. Even the development of photography, a child of modern times and a product of vastly changing technologies, got off on the wrong foot, not only because of the medium's poorly understood chemical processes but because of its rapidly developing popularity and its accessibility to the general public.

The aggregate result of these changes may now be seen in collections of modern holdings such as those gathered in the Harry Ransom Humanities Research Center. Paper is crumbling from the use of oxidizing bleaches to whiten the wood pulp; inks are fading because of the instability of the dyes from which they are made; modern leathers are disintegrating as a result of the use of poor-quality skins and more aggressive tanning procedures; and pressure-sensitive adhesives have chemically crosslinked, discolored, and dried out, no longer able to serve the purpose for which they were originally applied. Bookbindings have fallen apart because structurally they cannot handle the stresses of even moderate use, some being unable to stand upright on the shelves. Photographs have faded beyond recognition, and as a result of the instability of the materials from which they were prepared, some photographic collections, such as those containing nitrate film, have become major fire hazards for the buildings in which they are stored.

In 1980 Decherd Turner, Director of the HRHRC from 1980 to 1987, officially established a Conservation Department under the leadership of Don Etherington, who came to the University from the conservation program at the Library of Congress. It was the objective of the Center's Conservation Department to address the special problems associated with an archive of nineteenth- and twentieth-century collections. At the time that Don Etherington was appointed as Chief Conservation Officer and Assistant Director of the HRHRC, the development of conservation divisions within other American university libraries and special collections was not a widespread practice. Conservation departments had been established at the Newberry Library and at Yale and Harvard, and preservation programs were being considered and developed in a few other Ivy League universities as well as on the West Coast at Stanford. The Library of Congress conservation programs had been in place for more than a decade, and it was there that Etherington had participated in developing important new directions for the field of conservation.

Prior to his position with the Library of Congress, Etherington had studied bookmaking in England, both in the traditional indentured apprentice system and in the innovative workshop of Roger Powell. At the London County Council Central School of Arts—a school steeped in the tradition of William Morris—Etherington's teachers included William Matthews, Fred Wood, George Frewin, and Douglas Cockerell. In 1951 Etherington began a seven-year apprenticeship at Harrison and Sons in London, under the auspices of the Worshipful Company of Stationery and Newspaper Makers established by the Royal Charter in 1493. In 1958, after passing the City Guilds of London examinations, Etherington returned to Stationers' Hall with the status of freeman. His special job was designing full leather presentation bindings and boxes containing new stamp designs to be given to the Royal Family as gifts from Harrison and Sons. Feeling that he needed to broaden his experience in the field, Etherington left Harrison and Sons to work for the British Broadcast Corporation Music Library, where his job restoring sheet music was his first exposure to the field of restoration/conservation. During this time he began rebacking and restoring second-hand books under the tutelage of Howard Nixon, Keeper of Books at the British Museum. In 1959 Etherington joined Roger Powell and Peter Waters in their shop in Froxfield Village, Hampshire, where the emphasis was on the ability to understand the whole binding structure, not allowing trade practices or traditional styles to determine the decision-making process. After serving as a lecturer at the Southhampton College of Art from 1960 to 1970, Etherington joined the staff of the Library of Congress, where he served in the Conservation program from 1970 to 1980.

With Etherington's arrival at The University of Texas in 1980, it did not take long for the HRHRC administration to realize it had acquired more than simply a repairer of books and manuscripts. Conservators from the Library of Congress had been seasoned by ten years of administrative struggle in the development of their own conservation programs, and they were dedicated to the broader view of conservation within America's archives and libraries as a national crusade. They had become national spokespersons and leaders in the cry for conservation of our nation's literary and historical heritage, and Don Etherington was one of these leaders.

The small room assigned to the Conservation Department on the seventh floor of the Harry Ransom Center had been used previously as a bookbindery in 1973 by a Texas-trained bookbinder, Ron Peck, who established a small facility for the recasing and repair of items in the bound collections. Through the use of volunteers, Peck also developed a book oiling program and other stack maintenance procedures. Realizing that he needed further development and training in the skills of book conservation, Peck left the HRHRC for a year to attend a bookbinding training program in London, but on his return from England, he resigned from his position at the Center and established his own private practice in bookbinding.

The assumption that a nationally recognized Library of Congress conservator could be satisfied with a small seventh-floor workshop was soon corrected. Etherington's initial recruitment of a staff of three trainee book conservators, a secretary, and a volunteer trainee, and his acquisition of a large resource library and collection of bookbinding tools and equipment from a retired bookbinder, E.A. Thompson, stretched the limits of the area. Within a few months, the first in a series of expansionist relocations occurred. The Department moved to a three-thousand-plus square foot workshop area on the fifth floor, commandeered an office suite, and, eventually, through the use of temporary wall dividers annexed another one thousand square feet of space adjacent to the newly acquired workshop. But given the task facing the Department, one chief conservation officer and three trainee book conservators could not do it alone. By the end of 1980, Etherington had added to the staff a senior paper conservator, a senior book conservator, and a conservation scientist in photography. These conservators, in turn, required assistants to help carry the load, and thus several more trainee and assistant conservators were hired, primarily within the Paper Conservation Division. Volunteers, some with experience and some without, began to appear, strongly motivated to become involved with the development of the HRHRC conservation program.

Over the past eight years, approximately seventy persons have served in the Conservation Department in various capacities, either as full-time employees, interns, or part-time staff members. The majority of these persons received substantial amounts of training in conservation principles and practices while at the Center; some have stayed for very short periods and some have been with the Department for the duration. The senior paper conservator and current chief conservation officer both entered the department in 1981, and a conservator in the Book Conservation Section has been on the staff since 1980. The Conservation Department has always had a nearly equal mixture of personnel trained at the HRHRC and experienced staff trained prior to their coming to the University. This has been a purposeful policy adhered to by Etherington and one which is to some degree likely to continue, tempered slightly, perhaps, by the increased number of graduates of conservation training programs who are now becoming available.

At times the Conservation umbrella has sheltered such positions as a staff photographer, a registrar, a curatorial assistant, microfilmers, a grant writer, a photoduplication coordinator, an assistant director, an assistant to the director, and a scientist. As the winds of change are constant in the HRHRC, the

Department has recently begun to divest itself of many of the non-conservation functions which naturally fell its way as a result of Etherington's dual role as Chief Conservation Officer and Assistant Director of the Center.

After the move to the fifth floor in 1981, it became obvious that the conservation program had much to do in order to establish the procedures necessary to deal with the problems of the HRHRC collections. It was not enough simply to repair and conserve items if other aspects of their storage, use, and exhibition were not simultaneously addressed. A Ten Year Plan devised at the time by Etherington described the progress he anticipated could be made in the growth and responsibilities of the Department. It would require five years to establish the basic laboratory space, develop the fundamental preservation programs to address environmental needs and develop housing programs, and recruit and train a competent and professional staff necessary to support the development of a functioning conservation treatment program. The second five years of the program would see the addition of more highly skilled conservation staff, the development of more sophisticated conservation treatment facilities, and the establishment of well-defined collection treatment priorities. Throughout this projection there was a stated intent to develop an outreach program to educate archivists, librarians, and museum professionals within Texas and the Southwest in up-to-date preservation, exhibition, and conservation practices.

One of Etherington's first efforts was to involve the Center's staff in the conservation program. It was determined that, for a certain amount of time each week or month, all HRHRC staff members, whether in the Conservation Department or not, would engage in such preservation practices as the construction of phase boxes for the storage of rare books, the preparation of polyester book jackets, or the making of other types of storage containers for the protection of collection materials. While this idealistic sharing of the preservation effort could not last for long, the effect was of long-lasting importance in the awakening of the entire staff of the Center to the procedures involved in caring for the collections and why they were vital and even crucial. Departments such as the manuscripts cataloging section began to adopt numerous preservation practices into their daily routine and to adapt their housing systems to conservation precepts. Reading room staff set up areas for polyester jacketing of books, and staff members not engaged in other reading room activities pursued the construction of these protective jackets. The General Libraries Cataloging Department Stack Maintenance Unit, on permanent loan to the HRHRC, established a program for the routine construction of phase boxes of all bound items which were brought to their area for shelving. Photoduplication standards were established and guidelines for the care and copying of fragile or damaged materials were implemented. Within each of the curatorial divisions Photoduplication Coordinators were designated, and these persons served as liaisons with conservators to develop working methods for the protection of collection materials from damages caused in the process of creating microfilm, photocopy, and photographic records or copies. All of these programs continue in place up to the present time.

The HRHRC has always been active in the exhibition of its collections, and it did not take long for the curators of the Center to realize that a good conservation staff could produce extremely attractive exhibits. It also did not take long for the curators to realize that the Conservation Department had a number of strong opinions about how exhibitions should be managed. Of all the efforts of the conservation program the exhibition policies have been cause for the most debate and have resulted in the greatest overhaul of pre-1980 policies. An Exhibition Committee was appointed to control and approve all materials being requested for exhibition in the Center and for loan to other institutions. It was the purpose of this committee to determine the appropriateness of a loan request in light of the condition of the object, the exhibit requirements of the borrowing parties, and the environmental conditions at the proposed exhibition site. Charges for handling, preparation, and shipping were instituted and a registrar was hired to keep track of the paper work and to negotiate among the curators, the Conservation Department, and the exhibiting parties. The presence of a registrar elevated the exhibition and loan process to a level similar to that normally maintained by museums in their exhibition control and added an increased aspect of responsibility to the exhibition process. To keep track of the items, loan worksheets were developed which outlined policies for restricting the types of items that could be exhibited and the amount of time an item could be on display. To facilitate the preparation of collection materials for exhibition, a large room on the fourth floor of the Peter Flawn Academic Center, adjacent to the Iconography Collections storage areas, was established as the Exhibition Preparation Center. This facility, fully equipped for the hinging, matting, framing, and installation of works of art and photographs, was staffed by exhibition preparation personnel trained by the paper, book, and photographic conservators of the HRHRC.

In order to maintain a closer relationship with curatorial and cataloging activities within the Center's collections areas, the Conservation Department designated certain conservation personnel to serve as liaisons to the major HRHRC curatorial divisions: Manuscripts, Library, Photography, Theatre Arts, and Iconography. These liaisons created permanent "satellite workstations" within the curatorial areas, which became central to the interactions between the curatorial staff and the conservators regarding development of housing programs, selection of treatment priorities, implementation of surveys, and the maintenance of paperwork locating items consigned to conservation, preservation, or exhibition preparation. These stations also facilitated the ability of non-conservation staff to continue to expand their

WASHINGTONIANA

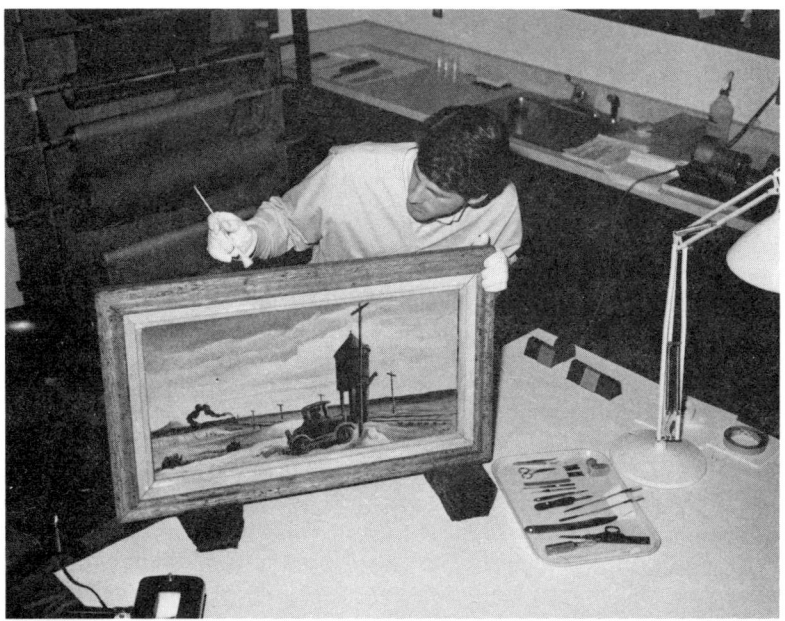

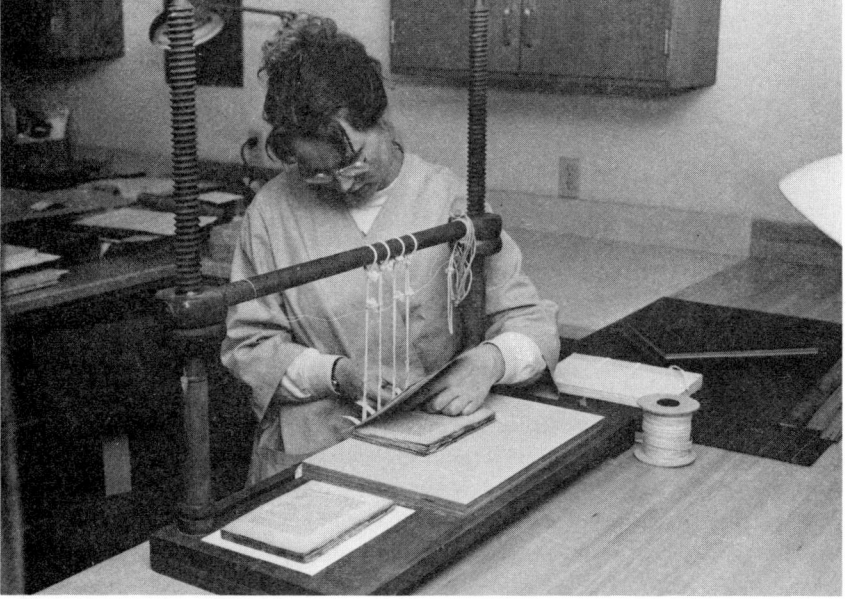

Above: Bruce Suffield, head of Exhibition Preparation, examines and dusts "Water Tank, West Texas," a tempera on canvas painting by Thomas Hart Benton from the HRHRC's Alfred A. and Blanche Knopf Library. Below: Mary C. Baughman, a book conservator, sews a textblock onto linen tapes at a traditional sewing frame.

involvement in preservation activities such as non-routine housing of collection artifacts and minor repair of tears and fractures with heat-activated adhesive-coated papers. Most importantly, these stations encouraged open dialogue between the conservators and the cataloging and curatorial staff. Conservation personnel who were appointed as the liaisons to the curatorial areas established more or less permanent residence at the satellite stations and inaugurated more advanced and innovative housing and preservation programs. Such personnel were relied on increasingly to assist with a wide variety of operations within their respective areas, such as assistance with small exhibits, preparation of items for shipping, inventory and recordkeeping, and identification of collection priorities for conservation treatment.

Problems with the establishment of conservation treatment priorities and with the allocation of conservation staff time to the various curatorial divisions were addressed through the creation of a Conservation Committee, which consisted of heads of the curatorial divisions and of the primary conservators associated with Books, Paper, Photographs, and Manuscripts. At the beginning of each year, the heads of the curatorial divisions were to develop a list of priorities which they would like for the conservators to address during the coming year. Working together with the conservators, they would then survey the requested projects to determine the amount of time the conservators estimated it would require for their completion. A project might involve a single item requiring conservation treatment or a large collection of materials requiring both treatment and preservation housing. Some projects would be approached in a progressively stepped or "phased" manner allowing initial work to be done in one year with more advanced levels to be completed at a later date. Time expended on projects was based on projections of available time embodied in the "conservation pie." This expedient subtracted the time reasonably expected to be spent by conservators on such matters as exhibition preparation, training of staff, public services, and general administrative duties. It was established that approximately fifty percent of any one conservator's worktime should be spent directly on priority conservation treatment work. This estimated length of time was then allocated to the individual curatorial areas based on a wide variety of factors, such as the need for the book conservation section to address conservation problems in all the major curatorial areas. Similar allocations were made for the proportion of time devoted to any one area by the paper and manuscript conservators. The "conservation pie" was divided each month to reveal the amount of time that was actually spent by the conservators in treatment situations and on which collections. This allowed the curators, as they became more familiar with how much the conservators could do in a given time, to assess more accurately their priorities.

Early in 1983 the Conservation Department made the last of a series of physical moves. The University of Texas Library School had been persuaded to relocate their facilities from the Harry Ransom Center to the Education and Psychology Building. This move freed half of the fourth floor of the Center, and the Conservation Department immediately vacated its fifth floor workspaces, moved to a small area on the fourth floor, and began renovation of the much larger areas which they were eventually to occupy. The renovation resulted in the establishment of three permanent conservation laboratories on the fourth floor. In addition to the three conservation labs, which service the photograph, manuscript and art on paper, and bound collections of the Center, there are also three preservation housing labs, two fully equipped exhibition preparation studios, a scientific equipment lab, a large resource center housing extensive conservation reference collections and treatment records, several small workrooms for such activities as working with solvents or preparing Plexiglas cradles for book and manuscript exhibits, a photographic studio, an exhibition area, a number of storage rooms for supplies and materials consumed by the preservation housing programs, an administrative office suite, and a row of offices for the conservation staff.

Throughout these developments in the conservation programs and the Department facilities, Etherington pursued his desire to develop and maintain outreach programs to other local and state repositories. From 1982 through 1986, the Department hosted Annual Conservation Seminars that drew archivists, librarians, curators, conservators, and collectors to the University for intensive three-day seminars, which featured workshops, lectures, and demonstrations. Manuals for the seminars were prepared for the participants, and the Center's conservation staff members were expected to produce articles for the manuals and to prepare workshops and lectures. The involvement of the staff members in these seminars has provided training and experience essential to their professional development as conservators, and lecture preparation and workshop demonstrations have improved their understanding of the issues with which they are involved on a daily basis. The seminars focused on various aspects of treatment, storage, and exhibition of books, manuscripts, art on paper, and photographs. In the 1986 Annual Seminar, entitled "The Conservation of Meaning," participants and conservation staff engaged in lively debate over issues related to changes caused to an artifact as a result of conservation treatment and how these changes might affect subsequent scholarly interpretation of the meaning of the artifact.

During 1987, the HRHRC established the Institute for Fine Bookbinding and Book Conservation. The objective of the Institute was to encourage advanced book conservators and binders to attend extended and intensive workshops in order to polish their professional skills under the instruction of prominent craftsmen and conservators. Two successful sessions of the Institute were held, each two months in duration. These sessions attracted many applicants, out of which twenty conservators and bookbinders from across the United States were chosen to attend and were provided with high-level training and in-depth experience in the areas of modern book design and the construction of medieval bindings in wooden boards. The first session was under the direction of James Brockman, a highly acclaimed bookbinder and designer from England. Mr. Brockman focused on techniques for executing fine bookbinding designs in leather, gold, and other media. The second session addressed the structure and construction of medieval bindings and was taught by Anthony Cains, the Chief Conservator at Trinity College in Dublin. During this program, the participants examined methods for shaping and attachment of oak boards to vellum manuscripts, for covering of boards with alum-tawed skin, and for shaping and attaching brass clasps to the boards.

In addition to the Annual Seminars and the Institute for Fine Binding and Book Conservation sessions, the Conservation Department has hosted numerous workshops, seminars, lectures, tours, and other educational events for such groups as the Rare Books and Manuscripts and the Preservation of Library Materials sections of the American Libraries Association, the Society of American Archivists, the Guild of Bookworkers, the Library Binding Association, and the Southwest Association for Conservation. Plans are currently being developed for a two-week preservation and conservation seminar for Latin American archivists, sponsored in conjunction with the National Archives and Records Administration and the Society of American Archivists, and to be hosted by the HRHRC in September of 1989.

It is important to expand the knowledge and experiences of the members of the Conservation staff through exposure to other conservators and to different ways of thinking about their work. The Conservation Department has actively encouraged conservators from other institutions and in private practice to visit the HRHRC and to present lectures and workshops for the staff. Internationally known conservators, who have visited the Center to discuss problems, to lecture, to hold workshops, or to participate in conservation projects with the Center's Conservation staff, include such well-respected names as Robert Futernick, Merrily Smith, Robert Feller, Chris Clarkson, Anthony Cains, Nicholas Pickwood, Hugo Peller, Tini Miura, Phillip Smith, Keiko Keyes, Sally Buchanan, James Reilly, Nathan Stolow, James Brockman, Peter Waters, Raymond Jordan, Jerri Cohn, Cathy Baker, Gisela Noack, Robert Espinosa, Ian and Angela Moor, Paul Banks, Gary Frost, Norvell Jones, and Nancy Terry, among numerous others. Currently under discussion is a proposal for Robert Espinosa, the Head of Conservation of the Harold B. Lee Library at Brigham Young University, to spend a six-week sabbatical working in the Center's Manuscript Conservation program beginning in June of 1989. Two prominent photographic conservators from England, Ian and Angela Moor, will spend four months during 1989 at the Center working with the photographic collections and training the staff in more advanced techniques for the conservation of photographs.

The Center's conservation program has established an outstanding reputation for professionalism because of its willingness to participate in a wide variety of national and international conservation programs. The conservation staff interacts with conservators throughout the world in efforts to promote public awareness of the critical issues of conservation and preservation. As a member of the National Institute for Conservation (NIC), the Center seeks to develop and refine better conservation treatment techniques for the care of our nation's cultural heritage and to encourage federal and state funding and support for programs designed to assist libraries, museums, and archives which do not have access to conservation facilities. Through its own training programs, as well as through the NIC and other agencies, the Center fosters the development of sound and effective programs for the education and training of new students of conservation and preservation. It is with a certain amount of pride that the HRHRC has continually had a strong and active presence at annual meetings of the American Institute for Conservation and at meetings of the International Institute of Conservation. Presentations by HRHRC conservators to the American Institute for Conservation and its various specialty groups have been well received. Most of the Conservation Department staff are active members of the American Institute for Conservation, the International Institute for Conservation, the Institute of Paper Conservation, and the Southwest Association for Conservation. Other affiliations within the department include membership in various sections of the American Library Association, the Society of American Archivists, the American Association of Museums, the International Institute for Conservation-Canadian Group, and the International Council of Museums.

The HRHRC Conservation Department continues to accept graduates and advanced students of library and museum conservation programs both in the United States and from abroad to serve three- to twelve-month internships at the Center. In return for conservation experience in a functioning laboratory under the guidance of the Center's professional conservators, these young conservators-in-training bring to the HRHRC their enthusiasm and new ideas developed through their training programs elsewhere. Such working relationships encourage valuable exchange of experiences and techniques between the visiting interns and the Center's conservation staff. Often these internships provide the final step in the students' training prior to their first professional employment. Simultaneously, the interns provide the Center with dedicated and willing hands to continue the battle against the deterioration of its irreplaceable collections. The willingness of the HRHRC to accept interns has been strongly supported by the Columbia University Library Graduate School Conservation Program; as of August 1988 five interns from the Columbia program have served internships with the HRHRC Conservation Department. During 1987 and 1988 the Center was fortunate in being able to work with two graduate conservation interns from the Columbia program, one of whom has recently been hired as a conservator in the Paper

Conservation lab. Currently an intern from the Conservation Training Program at the University of Paris is engaged in a nine-month internship with the Center's Paper Conservation Section.

At present there are thirteen full-time employees in the Conservation Department, along with several part-time volunteers and work-study staff. Among these personnel are five conservators servicing manuscripts, art on paper, photographs, and bound collections; five technical assistants servicing preservation needs of the curatorial divisions and the preparation of exhibitions; one administrative assistant responsible for safety concerns within the Center, the preservation housing programs, and the control and ordering of

Sue Murphy, senior paper conservator, removes an acidic backing from an ink drawing by Dante Gabriel Rossetti.

conservation and preservation supplies; and one very valuable office assistant/secretary/receptionist who serves in a multitude of capacities.

A full range of techniques are employed within the Conservation Department to protect and preserve the Center's extensive collection holdings. Working closely with HRHRC curators and administrators to identify priority items and collections for conservation treatment, the conservators apply such processes as the removal of art work and photographs from damaging supports or acidic mounting boards; the reduction of stains caused by poor-quality and inappropriate adhesives; the stabilization of chemical processes responsible for the embrittlement and discoloration of paper; the repair of historic and modern bookbindings; the reinforcement of paper weakened from the effects of fire, water, and mold; the consolidation of flaking media on paintings and illuminated manuscripts; and the stabilization of conditions responsible for the fading of photographic images. The hazards of exhibition are reduced through processes such as monitoring and control of light intensity, ultraviolet irradiation, temperature, and relative humidity in the exhibition galleries; archival hinging, matting, and framing techniques; careful attention to the construction of suitable shipping containers and the techniques of proper packing procedures; detailed examination and reporting of the condition of items before, during, and after exhibition; preparation of exhibition cradles to support weakened or fragile bindings; and establishment and recommendation of criteria for the duration of time which an item might safely be exhibited.

Members of the Conservation Department staff have assisted other institutions in recovery of collections which have been damaged because of flood, fire, or insect infestation. The maintenance of a Disaster Recovery Plan and the training of staff personnel to respond correctly during such emergencies are of paramount importance to the Center. Attendance by staff conservators at seminars and workshops devoted to Disaster Recovery is encouraged and the experiences gained through recovery assistance to other repositories ensure that the Center's Emergency Response Team will be well prepared in the event that an emergency situation threatens its own collections.

The articles that appear in this publication represent a diverse spectrum of the knowledge and skills which conservators must attain as they progress within their profession. Young conservators, such as Karen Pavelka and Carol Sue Whitehouse, who are both recent graduates of the Conservation Training Programs at Columbia University, have contributed articles about treatments which they pursued during internships at the HRHRC. These treatments were performed after careful analysis of the items to be treated and with direction and guidance from the experienced conservators on the staff responsible for their training and the quality of their work. The manuscript treatments reported by Ms. Pavelka and Ms. Whitehouse demonstrate two approaches to the ethical dilemmas presented by objects which, because of their own nature and structural characteristics, are a danger to themselves. The decisions to maintain or restructure physical formats related to the aesthetics, history, and provenance of the manuscripts revolve around these complex issues.

Not all the Center's conservators in training have been students of our nation's outstanding conservation training programs. Ellen Weir, who has recently accepted a position as an assistant conservator at the Northeast Document Conservation Center, was extensively trained on the job in the fashion of an apprentice by the HRHRC's manuscript and paper conservators. Her treatment of the Center's burned fragments of poetry by William Faulkner represents the serious responsibilities and the advanced level of control and skill which may be achieved during apprenticeship training under sensitive and concerned supervisors.

The role of the conservation technicians is of major importance to the HRHRC Preservation Programs. Jill Whitten, responsible for a wide range of housing exhibition and maintenance procedures, describes an internship at the University's Huntington Art Gallery in which she participated in a survey of painting collections. The experience she gained through this survey and subsequent treatments performed on the gallery's paintings under the supervision of the Huntington's conservator, Sarah McElroy, will improve the HRHRC Conservation Department's ability to care for its own large collections of paintings on canvas.

Mary Baughman's article discusses different approaches to the treatment of nineteenth-century publishers' case bindings and conveys the importance of careful decision-making in selecting from the many available options for the treatment of these delicate and often neglected and abused volumes.

The articles by Sue Murphy, Bruce Levy, and Barbara Brown are exemplary of the types of major treatments performed by advanced and seasoned conservators for such fields as art on paper, bookbinding, and photography. In their discussions of a storyboard, a fifteenth-century binding structure, and a nineteenth-century composite photograph, respectively, these three conservators reveal not only the complex issues involved in conservation treatment but the important scholarly and technical discoveries that are often made in the process of examining and treating items in the Center's varied collections.

An important article in this publication does not describe conservation treatment. Frank Yezer, in his discussion of the non-treatment options available for the preservation of collection materials, strikes at one of the most vital aspects of a conservation and preservation program such as this of the Harry Ransom Humanities Research Center: the importance of simple and straightforward techniques for the housing of items, whether of greater or lesser value, in good quality and archivally appropriate enclosures; and the necessity of an overall implementation of such practices by all levels of the Center's staff.

Ellen Cunningham-Kruppa, a graduate of the Columbia University Preservation Administration Program and at one time an employee of the HRHRC Manuscript Conservation Section, is now the Preservation Officer for the University's General Libraries. In her interim report on the General Libraries' Preservation Program, Ms. Cunningham-Kruppa describes the major problems involved in the preservation of large circulating collections within institutional libraries heavily used by researchers at both the undergraduate and graduate levels. Her article also makes clear the distinction between preservation programs for circulating collections and conservation programs for collections containing non-circulating rare books and manuscripts.

The preparation of these articles has been an unusual challenge for the Center's conservation staff. Conservators are required to produce extensive and detailed reports documenting the character and the condition of the objects they conserve and they are expected to describe fully all of the technical details of the procedures which they employ in their treatments of these objects. Such dry but informative reports are not always easy reading for a general audience. The idea of describing conservation treatments for a scholarly publication has provided numerous, and occasionally humorous, opportunities for the staff to reassess its literary style and has been the source of a number of interesting discussions between the authors and the editor. It is hoped that the final product of this somewhat bumpy endeavor will provide the reader with an understanding of the nature of the work of the conservation and preservation staff of the Harry Ransom Humanities Research Center, and of the General Libraries of The University of Texas, and that this publication will convey something of the ethical and technical issues involved in the care of our historic, literary, and artistic treasures.

The ability to impart technical information and procedures in a clear fashion to readers unfamiliar with the conservation field and its practices is a high priority for the Conservation Department of the HRHRC. By developing this ability, the Center's conservators are better able to communicate with their curators and administrators about conservation objectives and methodologies which may affect the intrinsic meaning of collection items being considered for conservation treatment. Equally important, the conservators of the HRHRC will be better able to establish a meaningful public dialogue leading towards the overriding goal of long-term preservation of the treasures held within the Center in the name of the public whose funds mandate and support this goal. For in part, those who have entrusted their cultural heritage to the care of the HRHRC depend on the Center's ability and commitment to protect its collection for the future use and enjoyment not only of the people of the State of Texas but of the entire world.

—James Stroud
Chief Conservator, HRHRC

Painted by T. Phillips in 1814 and engraved by Y. Lufton in 1824, this mezzotint of Lord Byron was tipped in to the flyleaf of the bound manuscript of *The Siege of Corinth*. HRHRC Collections.

Conservation Treatment of a Bound Manuscript in the Byron Collection

BY KAREN PAVELKA

A large collection of Byroniana at the Harry Ransom Humanities Research Center includes manuscripts, letters, and associated materials, the majority of which came to the University of Texas in 1938 as part of the Miriam Lutcher Stark library.[1] Significant additions to the collection were made in 1941 by Mrs. Stark's son, H.J. Lutcher Stark. In 1947 the University acquired a group of letters mainly relating to the Pisan Affray, and in the same year Willis W. Pratt published *Lord Byron and His Circle*, a "Calendar of Manuscripts" listing the contents of the University's Byron Collection.[2] Only minor additions have been made to the collection since the compilation of Pratt's "Calendar." Of the more than 70 Byron letters and documents and more than 30 manuscripts of his poems in the HRHRC collection, a number have never been published. In addition to the Lord Byron items, the collection also comprises letters by Lady Byron and by other figures associated with the poet's life, as well as nearly all of Byron's printed works in first and later editions.

In reviewing the Byron materials at the HRHRC, John Kirkpatrick, head of the Center's Manuscript Department, designated the Byron manuscripts as a priority for conservation treatment. After a brief survey was conducted to identify conditions which might threaten individual works if left untreated, it was found that the majority of the problems fell into two categories: first, works that had received improper treatment in the past; and second, those that required more adequate protective housing than had been provided previously. An example from the first category is the group of twenty-five leaves that constitutes the Center's manuscript copy of Lord Byron's *The Siege of Corinth*, which was begun by the poet in 1812, a version of which was

---

[1]The Stark library was acquired in 1925, but the manuscript of Byron's *The Siege of Corinth* (Stark number 6535) did not come to the University of Texas until 1938.

[2]*Lord Byron and His Circle: A Calendar of Manuscripts in the University of Texas Library*, compiled by Willis W. Pratt (Austin, 1947). *The Siege of Corinth* is item number 75 and is described on pages 23-24.

was first published in 1816.[3] A fashionable practice in the late nineteenth century was to bind such manuscripts, often quite elaborately, in what were known as "extra" bindings.[4] These bindings have frequently proved harmful to the contents because of their structures and the poor quality of their materials. It can be argued that binding was not the original intent of the author, and certainly in the case of this manuscript the binding was causing damage to the manuscript leaves.

Although Lord Byron is known to have begun his writing of *The Siege of Corinth* in 1812, the HRHRC's copy is dated on the first page "J[anuar]y 30th, 1815." By the time of its acquisition by the University in 1938, the leaves of Byron's manuscript, originally in folio sheets, had been slit at the folds in order to be bound together with a printed text of the poem. Both the binding and the printed poem date from the period between the 1840s and 1880s, and according to HRHRC librarian John P. Chalmers, the volume was probably printed and bound at the same time, since the printed text faces line-for-line the text of the manuscript leaves inlaid on opposing pages. A fair copy of the poem, which was made by Lady Byron and sent to the publisher John Murray, remains the property of the Murray descendants. The HRHRC's manuscript of *The Siege of Corinth*, which begins at line 46 of the text printed in 1816, was in the hands of the poet and his descendants, but the exact details of its provenance are not known.[5] In 1885, the future Baron Glenesk acquired the Piccadilly house where Byron had lived while he was writing *The Siege of Corinth*. Although Lord Glenesk was not noted as a collector of books or manuscripts, he may have acquired the manuscript of Byron's poem because it had been written in the Piccadilly house. On 26 July 1910, the manuscript

---

[3]Pratt indicates that the HRHRC's version of the poem was not published until 1830. A Sotheby sale catalogue description pasted to the verso of the front endleaf of the HRHRC's bound volume states that this manuscript "differs in many respects from the version published in 1816, which was printed from a transcript in Lady Byron's handwriting."

[4]"Extra binding" is "a binder's term for a copy which has been bound and 'finished' (i.e. lettered and decorated) in the most elegant style (saving, of course, *super-extra*), with all edges gilt and usually a good deal of gilt decoration. While applicable to any kind of leather, it is used chiefly of MOROCCO bindings." See John Carter, *ABC for Book Collectors*, sixth edition, with corrections and additions by Nicholas Barker (London: Granada, 1982), p. 92.

[5]According to the Sotheby's description, the HRHRC manuscript "begins at line 46, the first 45 lines, which are introductory, having been sent to Murray sometime afterwards, and not published until 1830." The bookseller refers to E.H. Coleridge's belief that the manuscript consists "of portions of two or more fair copies of a number of detached scraps written at various times, together with two or three of the original scraps (Byron, Works, Poetry, vol. III, 1900)," but the bookseller remarks that contrary to Coleridge's view "the corrections and erasures on every page are so numerous that it is difficult to believe that any earlier version ever existed." According to the bookseller's description, the HRHRC's manuscript "is the earliest and only original autograph MS. of the Poem that survives."

Front cover of *The Siege of Corinth* manuscript, bound in dark-blue leather with gold tooling.

was offered as lot 198 at Sotheby's Miscellaneous Sale, and the clipped bookseller's description designates the item as "The Property of a Lady," who was Lilias Margaret Francis, Lord Glenesk's only heir. Purchased by the famous bookdealer Frank T. Sabin, the manuscript subsequently passed to Miriam Lutcher Stark of Orange, Texas, in 1922, and later to the University of Texas.

In September 1987, the bound volume of Byron's *The Siege of Corinth* was brought to the HRHRC's conservation lab for assessment and possible treatment. A variety of problems from a structural and chemical standpoint suggested that it was in the best interest of the manuscript that it be removed from the bound volume. While removal of the manuscript leaves from the binding would improve their long-term stability, this had to be weighed against changing the format of an historical artifact. With the Byron volume, the question was whether the manuscript should be considered as an independent artifact or as a critical element of another structure.

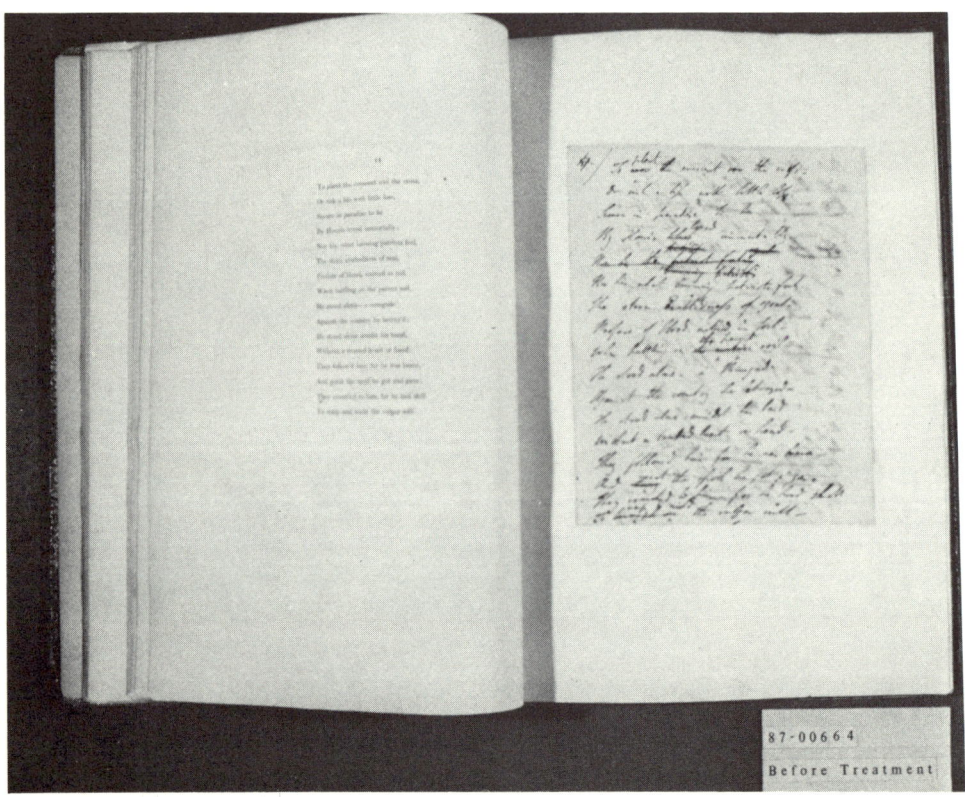

Open volume showing a manuscript leaf inlaid to face its corresponding printed text.

The American Institute for Conservation of Historic and Artistic Works, which is the professional group for conservators in North America, has produced a code of ethics for the treatment of such artifacts as the Byron volume. The AIC maintains that conservators should respect the integrity of an object being treated. "Intervention" is warranted if it is to prevent damage from occurring, or if it is to restore an object to its original condition prior to a previous treatment. A decision to treat an object is usually not made unless the artifact would suffer if it were not treated. In a library situation, the ideal of limited intervention by the conservator is continually at battle with the need to make materials accessible to the public. In order to be useful, library materials must be handled, and merely to preserve the original format can at times leave an artifact too fragile to be handled by a library patron. Yet if the object cannot be handled, then it can be argued that the artifact is not being preserved at all, but fossilized.

DESCRIPTION OF THE MANUSCRIPT

The HRHRC's manuscript leaves of *The Siege of Corinth* were inlaid and bound in dark-blue grained leather in a renaissance arabesque style with gold tooling. All edges are gilt. Endbands, which it can be assumed were once present, are now missing. A bookmark of blue silk is detached from the spine, while part of a binder's ticket remains attached to the upper left corner of the front pastedown, although the name of the binder is missing. The collective leaves of a bound volume are referred to as the textblock, which in this case is a folio in fours with the collation 2°: A^4 $B-N^4$; *1-104*pp.[6] An introduction to the poem was written in graphite pencil on the recto of the flyleaf and a mezzotint of Lord Byron was tipped in to the verso of the flyleaf. In each section, leaves 1 and 3 are printed text, and leaves 2 and 4 have inlaid manuscript leaves corresponding to the printed text.

It is clear from the assemblage of these materials and the manner of their presentation that late-nineteenth-century owners cherished such volumes. However, in the case of the Lord Byron manuscript, its elaborate binding, instead of protecting the volume, was creating problems because of the weakened binding structure and the poor quality of its materials. The spine was heavily consolidated with glue, which caused it to become stiff and prevented it from opening easily. From being pared very thin, the leather of the joints had grown increasingly fragile with age and thus susceptible to breakage. The joints of this volume were so weakened that the front board had become detached from the binding. In general, the leather of the late

---

[6]This collation formula is written according to the rules found in Philip Gaskell's *A New Introduction to Bibliography* (Oxford: Clarendon Press, 1972).

nineteenth century is often weak and subject to "red rot."[7] Also, the paper of this period is often of an inferior quality and consequently becomes brittle with age and tends to crack instead of flexing.

As the nineteenth-century demand for paper dramatically increased, wood pulp, already in use as a papermaking fiber by the early 1800s, began to replace cotton and linen fibers in paper. By the late nineteenth century, most paper was machine-made and has generally proved inferior to handmade paper for a variety of reasons. In the first place, papermaking machines work most efficiently when the pulp used has short fibers, but short fibers make for a weaker paper than do long fibers. Although wood pulp can provide a high quality paper when properly processed and treated, certain processing methods produced a pulp that contains lignin, which is the component of wood that "cements" the plant fibers. As lignin degrades, it produces acids that can break down the cellulose molecule into smaller particles, so that if it is not removed, lignin can cause paper to degrade rapidly.

The Byron volume is composed of five different papers, which include four handmade manuscript papers and one machine-made paper for the textblock. While all the manuscript papers proved to be of high quality and were still in good, flexible condition, the textblock leaves were becoming brittle, inflexible, and prone to cracking along the gutter. The yellowing around the edges of the textblock was an indication that its machine-made paper was degrading and becoming brittle. In turn, darkening and brittleness of the paper are indications that it is in the acidic range. Damage to the inlaid manuscript leaves had been caused by an impression left on them from the printed sheets as a result of the pressure applied to the book during the binding process. Also, the manuscript leaves were at risk while remaining in the volume because the handmade papers flexed differently from the machine-made paper of the printed text. When each page was turned, a tenting effect was created, sometimes leaving small dent impressions on the manuscript leaves. Further damage to a better quality handmade paper can also result from contact with such an acidic, machine-made sheet when acid from one migrates to the other. In addition, the adhesive used for the inlaying had begun to darken and become brittle, and in some areas it showed through the manuscript leaves. Again, the darkening and brittleness indicated that the paper was probably in the acid range. It was clear, therefore, that the

---

[7]"Red rot" is the common term for "a type of deterioration of leather (bookbindings), which generally takes two forms: 1) a hardening and embrittling of the leather, which occurs most often in leathers up to about 1830, i.e., books published (or at least bound) up to that date, and which is especially noticeable in calfskin bindings; and 2) a powdering of the leather, which can be so severe as to destroy it completely. This latter deterioration appears to affect virtually all leathers. . . ." See Matt T. Roberts and Don Etherington, *Bookbinding and the Conservation of Books: A Dictionary of Descriptive Terminology* (Washington, D.C.: Library of Congress, 1982), p. 214, under "red decay."

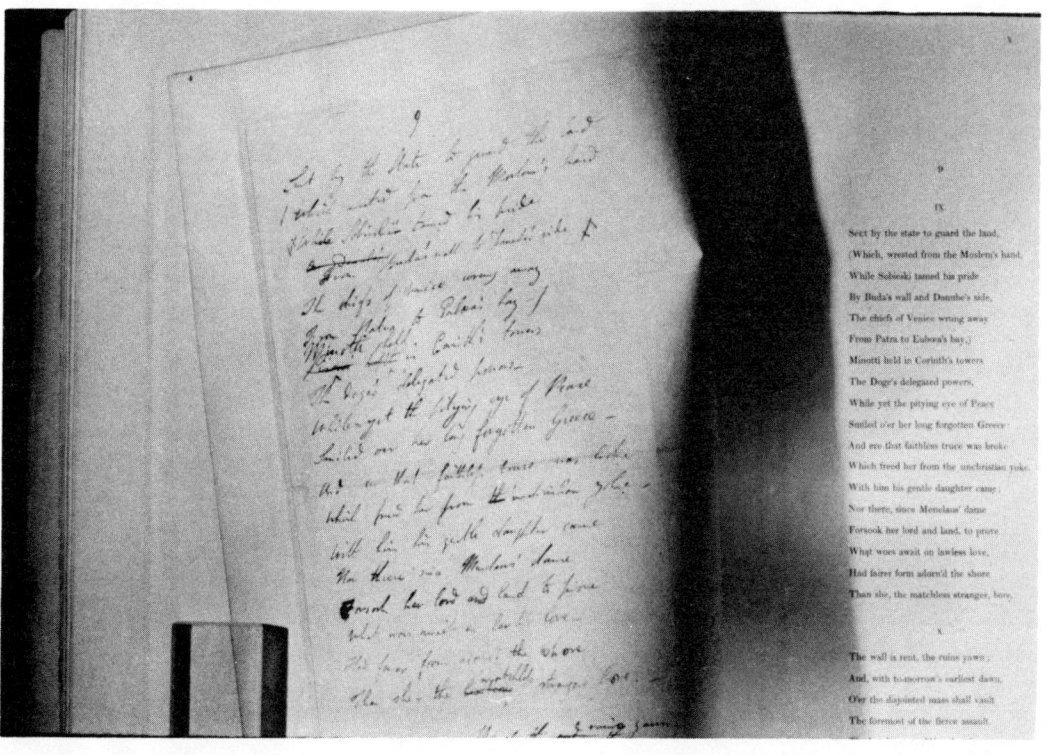

Open volume showing tenting effect caused when pages were turned, owing to the difference in flexibility between the manuscript leaves and the machine-made paper.

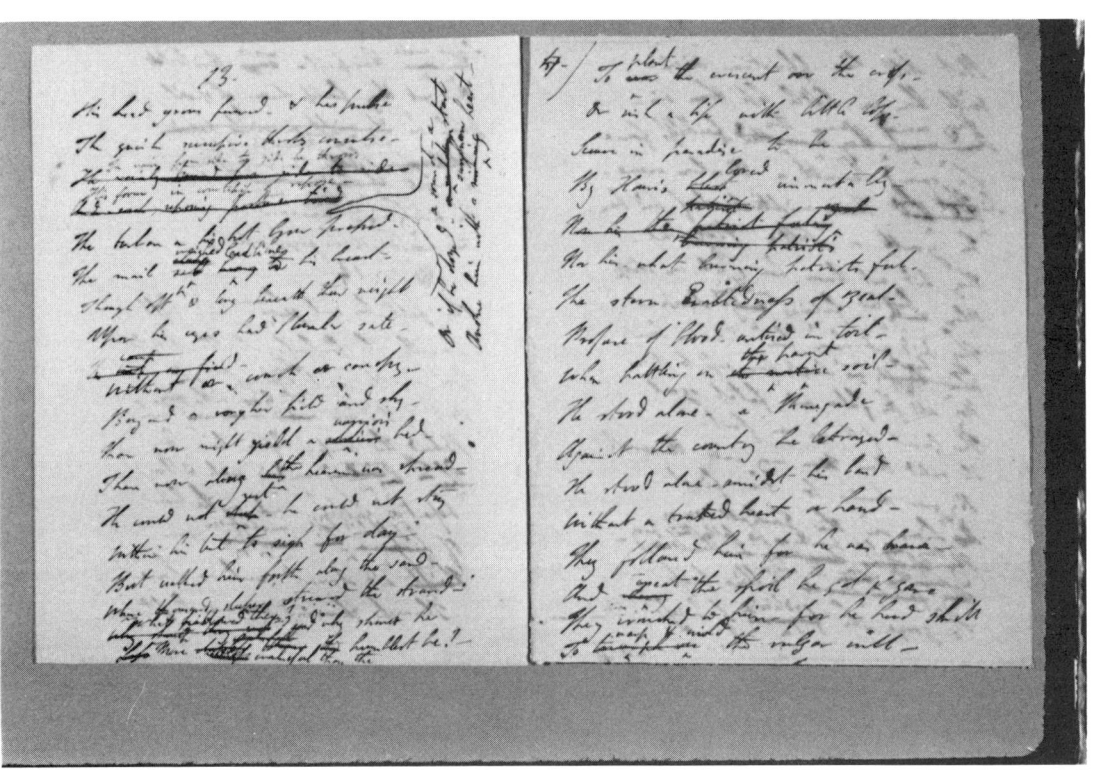

Originally these sheets were two leaves of the same folio but were split in order to be inlaid. The leaf on the left is shown after being washed in two baths of distilled water and one of distilled water with enough ammonium hydroxide to bring the bath to a pH of 9. Before the two leaves were washed, both were the same color; afterwards, both exhibited a lighter tone from the darkened color of the manuscript leaf pictured here on the right. The color and intensity of the ink, however, was unaffected by this treatment.

manuscript leaves should be removed from contact with the textblock sheets. Even though in taking this decision the character of the bound volume would be altered drastically, the permanent damage to the manuscript was considered more crucial than the preservation of the binding.

Treatment Objectives

The primary objective of the conservation treatment of the Byron bound volume was to remove its manuscript leaves and place them in a more benign environment. Even though an effort would be made to preserve the binding after the manuscript had been removed, the value of the binding was not considered great enough to warrant the time required to restore it completely to its original condition. No attempt would be made at repairing the broken gutter margins of the pages or at reattaching the front board or the silk marker. Thus, in dismantling the bound volume, care would be taken to protect the manuscript in preference to the binding. However, in order to make possible the continued use of the bound volume, steps would be taken to prevent further degradation of the textblock of the printed text and precautions would be taken against further damage to the cutout inlay sheets.

Treatment Procedures

Prior to conservation treatment, the condition of an artifact is fully documented by a written and a photographic record. In the case of the Byron bound volume, slides were taken of the binding, each leaf of *The Siege of Corinth* manuscript, recto and verso, as well as representative slides of the printed text. Once the manuscript leaves had been removed from the binding, they were photocopied, recto and verso. Photocopying provides a record of tears and stains that can be checked quickly and easily during the course of the treatment.

Once the artifact is fully documented, its components are tested to aid in determining how to proceed with treatment. Testing of the adhesive holding the manuscript leaves to the textblock showed it to be water soluble. Likewise, the writing ink used on the manuscript was found to be extremely soluble in water. In some areas along the interface between the manuscript and the inlay paper, the textblock paper covered handwriting, creating a problem in detaching one paper from another. Also, since the manuscript leaves absorbed water more quickly than the textblock paper, it would not be possible to apply water only to the textblock in order to break the adhesive holding the two sheets together. This meant that removal of the textblock paper would have to be achieved mechanically by careful scraping, as far as possible, without the aid of moisture to soften the adhesive. The few paper fibers remaining on the manuscript leaves would be removed with small, carefully controlled amounts of water, avoiding any prolonged contact of moisture with the ink.

In testing the inks, a slightly damp piece of blotter was held in contact with the ink for increasing lengths of time. Although an immediate transfer was observed of the ink onto the blotter, if the same area was tested repeatedly, eventually there was no longer an off-set and no change was visible in the appearance of the ink. This was repeated in several different areas of each manuscript paper. It is likely that the components which bled from the Byron manuscript were of a dye rather than of the ferric iron salt of the ink. The manuscript ink was recognized as iron gallotannante, which was probably used as far back as the eleventh century. Made by dissolving iron salt (ferrous sulphate) in an infusion of nutgalls, with plant gum or glue added as a binder, iron gallotannante turns black over time, caused by oxygen from the air acting upon the iron salt. The salt changes from ferrous, which is easily soluble and not intensely colored, to ferric, which is black and nearly insoluble in water. When the liquid was initially applied to paper it was transparent, or had only a very faint color. The practice of adding dyes to the mixture to make the ink immediately visible began in the late eighteenth century, with logwood extract and indigo among the dyes that were used. Since the ink of the Byron manuscript did not depend on the dyes for its intensity, this would account for the fact that the color was unchanged visibly with repeated applications of the damp blotter.

After testing the inks, the manuscript leaves were cut from the volume, leaving approximately an eighth-inch border of textblock paper. Working on a light table with knives and tweezers, the textblock paper was cautiously peeled away as much as possible. Working with each leaf on a light table, that is, a flat, rigid surface through which a soft, even light shines, the light transmitted through the paper allowed for observation of any disturbance of the fibers. Although the manuscript paper was in good, flexible condition, each face of each sheet had been in direct contact with the brittle and acidic textblock paper over a long period of time. Even when the manuscript sheets were freed from the bound volume, they retained a musty odor, characteristic of old, acidic paper. Therefore, it was believed that washing the manuscript would benefit the leaves.

Washing paper in water has been shown to improve its physical condition, both the color and strength. This process removes some of the grime accumulated from handling and storage, removes the water-soluble acid degradation products, and may strengthen the paper by reestablishing some of the hydrogen bonding between molecules. An alkaline rinse can further improve paper qualities by eliminating more of the acidic degradation products. Since most soils and natural stains are acidic, alkaline washing solutions counteract these more effectively than non-alkaline solutions.

The top photograph shows the weights used to press the new fill sheets into the holes created when the manuscript leaves were removed. At the bottom, the open volume is shown with the fill sheet that replaced the manuscript leaf.

Ammonium hydroxide in water is often a preferred cleaning agent, owing to its volatility, which means that it will not leave a residue from the rinse.

Washing is best carried out in very pure water, that is, water without any contaminants. Most city tap water is unsuitable for such treatment since it contains ions that are associated with the degradation of paper. Some ions are suspected of playing a role in what is commonly known as "foxing," which can be recognized by the small reddish-brown spots which sometimes occur on aged papers. These spots are not entirely understood, but they may be the result of the reaction catalyzed by metallic ions. Therefore, the distilled water used in the HRHRC's conservation lab is piped to the Center, and to campus science labs, from the University's Physical Plant, which distills water for such special uses.

Acid, which is the greatest threat to paper, is introduced from a number of sources. The papermaking process can employ bleaches and alum rosin size, although it is unlikely that either one was used in the manuscript papers of the Byron volume. In the case of the textblock paper, both ingredients were probably introduced, as suggested by the brittleness of the sheets, which indicated a high acid content. Contact between the two papers would have caused acid to be transferred from the textblock to the manuscript leaves. Acid can also be introduced from the air, since in most urban environments there is a high component of sulphur dioxide and other pollutants that can be absorbed by paper. The major component of paper is cellulose, which is a relatively stable molecule, insoluble in water and unaffected by dilute alkali. However, cellulose is subject to attack by acid and strong alkalis. The cellulose fibers in paper are held together by hydrogen bonding and other forces, but acid hydrolysis degrades the cellulose polymer, resulting in a decreased degree of polymerization, or chain length of the cellulose molecule. This means that the molecule is shortened, and as this occurs, the paper becomes weakened and brittle, usually darkening in color. The degradation of the cellulose molecule is a self-perpetuating reaction that produces acidic components, which in turn encourage further degradation.

There are various ways to monitor the condition of paper. The degree of polymerization can be measured by treating the cellulose with a strong alkali and measuring the viscosity of the resulting solution. This is necessarily a destructive test, and it is therefore not appropriate for an artifact. Condition can also be monitored by measuring the pH, the concentration of hydrogen and hydroxyl ions in a solution. A higher concentration of hydroxyl ions means a solution is more alkaline, whereas a higher concentration of hydrogen ions indicates that a solution is acidic. A scale of 1 to 14 is used to measure pH, with the acidity level ranging from 1 to 7, the alkalinity from 7 to 14, and 7 considered neutral. Since this is a logarithmic function, the farther from the neutral point, the greater the difference in strength between integers. That is, the increase of acidity is proportionally greater between pH3 and pH4 than between pH4 and pH5, just as the increase of alkalinity is proportionally greater between pH8 and pH9 than between pH7 and pH8. In treating paper, the object is to reduce the level of acidity to a reading closer to a neutral or alkaline point on the scale.

As a document goes through treatment, paper conservators routinely monitor the changes in its pH level. There are two ways to measure the pH of a sheet of paper: hot or cold extraction, which requires the destruction of a small sample of the paper; or surface pH, which requires that an electrode be in contact with a wet piece of paper for a period of time, ranging from several seconds to several minutes. For obvious reasons, only the second method is used, but it can be argued that surface pH measurement is at best imprecise, essentially because pH is a wet measurement and paper is dry. (When a pH reading is taken, one is not actually measuring the pH of the paper but the pH of the water-soluble components in the paper as they dissolve.) Comparative tests show that there is a discrepancy between surface pH and pH by extraction, especially as the measurement approaches and enters the alkaline range, which can be attributed to acids and alkalis with low solubility or those attached to the cellulose molecule. Nonetheless, to monitor the pH by a surface reading over the course of a treatment, though not a precise measurement, is indicative of trends. It is also helpful in keeping accurate records of every treatment performed should it become necessary to treat objects again at some point in the future, for many problems in conservation today have arisen due to imperfect records of past treatments.

In monitoring the Byron manuscript, it was found that the leaves had a relatively low pH when they were first removed from the binding. Although the manuscript leaves registered between 3.7 and 4.6, which was well within the acid range, it was feared that washing them would involve a risk to the inks that had proved to be water-soluble, or that contained at least one water-soluble component. However, it was felt that the low pH was dangerous to the stability of the paper and that by washing the leaves this level could be raised. Thus, the decision was made to wash the sheets. Part of the reasoning was that the appearance of the manuscript would not change visibly. Even if it had changed, the decision might have been made in favor of washing, since manuscripts must be viewed on their own terms and not as art objects. Changing the hue of a drawing is a more drastic consequence than changing that of a manuscript. In considering Byron's autograph manuscript, the visibility of the words, the emendations, and the other marks on the paper are of greater importance than the tone of the ink. Since leaving the paper in a degraded condition could ultimately damage the legibility of the writing, washing was therefore beneficial to the continued life of the manuscript leaves.

Washed first in distilled water, the leaves were removed from the bath, air dried, and then washed again. Afterwards, the leaves were washed a third time in a bath to which a small amount of ammonium hydroxide was added. Only about one drop of ammonium hydroxide was used in a large tray of water, but this was enough to raise the pH of the bath to between 9.0 and 9.5, which would counteract the acidity. The pH of the paper was monitored over the course of the treatment, and was found to rise to between 5.6 and 6.6. Although this is not a neutral or alkaline point, further sample washing did not indicate that the pH would rise significantly.

When washing of the manuscript leaves was complete, major tears were mended using Japanese tissue and wheat starch paste. Japanese tissue, which is commonly used as a mending material, has been proved a strong and durable paper. Minor tears—those less than approximately a thirty-second of an inch—were not mended since, ultimately, the leaves were to be housed in clear polyester sleeves, which would protect small tears during their use by library patrons.

One way of classifying paper into two broad categories is to distinguish between Western and Japanese. These names, though not definitive, have come into common usage because of the differing materials and methods from and by which the two types of paper are fabricated. Western paper traditionally was made from either cotton or linen fibers, whereas Japanese paper is traditionally made primarily from kozo, gampi, or mitsumata, which are bast fibers, meaning that they are taken from just below the bark layer of the particular plant. Around the turn of the century, after a period of extensive experimentation with different fibers, most Western papers began to be made from wood fibers, although some of the better quality papers were still made from cotton, with linen used only for a very few specialty papers. In the case of Japanese paper, the bast fibers are processed in such a manner that they remain very long, thus making possible the production of a paper that is thin but still extremely strong. Japanese paper is generally much thinner than Western paper, and suitable for making mends that are almost invisible. Modern Japanese papers sometimes incorporate some wood pulp mixed in with the traditional bast fibers, but in many cases these are still strong papers.

The Byron manuscript was probably written on folio sheets, which were slit for the purpose of inlaying them in the textblock windows. There are two types of papers that were used for the manuscript leaves: laid and wove.[8] Manuscript leaves 1-4 and 11-22 are of a medium weight, off-white handmade

---

[8] "Laid" and "wove" are terms used to identify certain visual characteristics of paper. Paper is made by casting a dispersion of pulp in water onto a screen and draining the water from it. Any texture of the screen is visible in the finished sheet of paper. Traditional papermaking molds were made with a mesh of parallel wires, tied together at intervals by perpendicular wires in a chain stitch. The intervals were not always the same. The lines resulting from the narrow wires are wire or laid lines, and those from the widely spaced wires, chain lines. Paper with chain and laid lines is referred to as "laid." Watermarks are fabricated by the same principle, working a raised design onto the mold with wire. Wove paper has a smooth overall appearance, resulting from a mesh stretched across the mold to disguise the chain and laid lines.

laid paper with a blue-green cast, measuring approximately 327 x 205mm. Manuscript leaf 1 is slightly wider than the other leaves of the same paper, with a crease approximately 15mm from the left edge (recto), which would have been the center crease of a folio sheet. The chain lines of this paper are approximately 26mm apart and there are 10 laid lines to 10mm. Since the chain lines match up, this indicates that originally these sixteen leaves were eight folio sheets. An elaborate watermark of an allegorical representation of Britannia is present on these leaves, as well as a countermark ALLEE 1813.[9]

Manuscript leaves 5-8 are of a medium weight, off-white wove handmade paper with a yellowish cast and no watermark, each approximately 223 x 180mm. Manuscript leaves 6 and 8 bear the watermark WARD & MIDDLETON 1812. Manuscript leaves 9 and 10 are of a medium weight, off-white wove handmade paper with no watermark. Manuscript leaves 23-25 are of a medium weight, off-white wove handmade paper, with a yellow-green cast, bearing the watermark J WHATMAN 1814. The orientation of manuscript leaf 25 is horizontal rather than vertical. Although there are no marks to be matched on the wove papers, it is possible that the wove leaves were split from folio sheets in order to be inlaid and bound. The sequence of the papers also suggests that they were once folios, since like papers occur throughout the volume in groups of even numbers of pages, except for the last group, which has an extra odd leaf. In the corners of the manuscript leaves are pinholes that were created to facilitate the inlaying process. When the rectangles were cut from the textblock leaves, the pinholes were lost, but their placement was documented and is still visible on photocopies.

Rather than mending the Byron manuscript leaves into their original configuration of folio sheets, they were encapsulated individually in clear polyester film. The sheets were intended for library use and polyester is suitable for handling and for the long-term storage of such paper artifacts, since this clear film has been shown to be an inert material that will protect the paper without contributing to its degradation. Also, encapsulating the leaves in polyester would not place any strain on the mends and would make possible the alignment of chain and laid lines with the use of a light table. A label indicating pagination was encapsulated at the top of each package, with a seal between the manuscript leaf and the label. The sealed packages were then housed in manuscript boxes.

---

[9]A watermark is "a distinguishing mark or device incorporated in the wire mesh of the tray in which the pulp settles during the process of papermaking, and visible in the finished product when held against the light. The maker's name or initials, the place or date of manufacture, if added, were more apt to be embodied in the *countermark*, a subsidiary and smaller unit introduced in the 17th century, generally placed in the opposite half of the sheet to the watermark proper. The presence of a watermark is normal in 'laid' paper, rarely found in 'wove' paper used for book printing." See Carter, *ABC for Book Collectors*, p. 214.

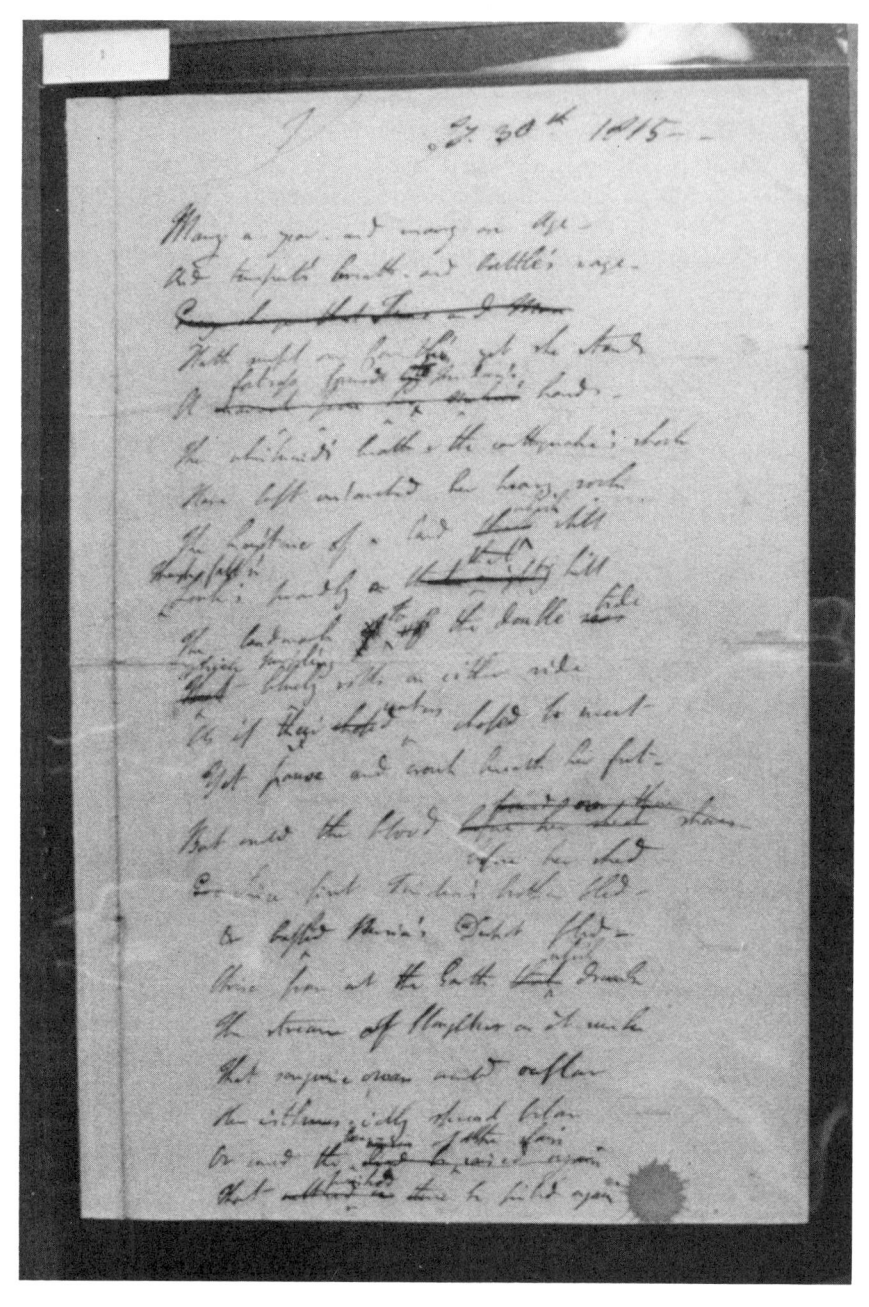

Final housing of a Byron manuscript leaf in a polyester envelope sealed on all sides, with pagination label in upper left corner.

Restoring the Bound Volume

The partial restoration of the bound volume was carried out by cutting sheets of Howard Mill Permalife Bond paper to a size just slightly larger than the holes in the inlay sheets. The edges of the bond paper were then pared, paste was applied, and the new fill sheet pasted over the hole. Each sheet was dried under weight, and when all the sheets had been filled, the entire volume was left in a press for a week. No further restoration was performed, and the reconstructed bound volume was stored separately from the encapsulated manuscript leaves.

Conclusion

Although it cannot be denied that the character of the artifact has been altered from what it was when first acquired by the Center, both the manuscript and the bound volume can now be used for research without serious danger to either. The manuscript leaves are well protected by a strong polyester film, through which both the recto and verso of each leaf are visible and by means of which the chain and laid lines of each can be aligned with the other leaves. The bound volume can also be requested by HRHRC patrons as a separate item, even though the brittleness of its pages and the fragility of its binding will dictate that handling be kept to a minimum.

Coverjacket of D.H. Lawrence's *The First Lady Chatterley* (London: Heinemann, 1972). Jacket illustration by Larry Learmonth. *HRHRC Collections*.

D.H. Lawrence's "The First Lady Chatterley": Conservation Treatment of a Twentieth-Century Bound Manuscript

BY CAROL SUE WHITEHOUSE

D.H. Lawrence began writing *Lady Chatterley's Lover* in October 1926 at Villa Mirenda outside Florence, Italy, and by the end of January 1928 he had completed in longhand three versions of the novel and had begun a typescript version for publication.[1] In a letter dated 4 February 1928, Lawrence wrote to Harold T. Mason: "I'm going over my novel here—the typescript—and I'm going to try to expurgate and substitute sufficiently to produce a properish public version, for Alf Knopf, presumably, to publish."[2] It appears that Lawrence recognized early on that this novel would be controversial and that it would encounter the same difficulties in being published as had some of his earlier works. The handwritten versions of *Lady Chatterley's Lover*, produced before Lawrence began expurgating the novel to make it "properish," represent important artifacts that provide evidence of the author's writing process and the development of his prose style. All three longhand versions of *Lady Chatterley's Lover* form part of the D.H. Lawrence Manuscript Collection at the Harry Ransom Humanities Research Center and have been the subject of extensive scholarly examination. Unfortunately, the first of these versions, "The First Lady Chatterley," already fragile, was potentially in danger of further damage from continued routine scholarly use.

Acquired from the New York bookdealer Lew David Feldman, "The First Lady Chatterley" came to the HRHRC in 1965, along with the two subsequent longhand versions and a quarto-sized privately printed version of Lawrence's novel.[3] Handwritten in manuscript ink on paper with blue, pen-ruled lines, the manuscript leaves were bound in a case binding whose boards had become detached from the textblock. Documents pertaining to the sale of

---

[1] Keith Sagar, *D.H. Lawrence: A Calendar of His Works* (Austin: University of Texas Press, 1979), pp. 153-154.

[2] D.H. Lawrence, *The Centaur Letters* (Austin: University of Texas Press, 1970), p. 32.

[3] Information on the acquisition of these materials is found in the vertical file of the HRHRC Special Collections under the heading of Lawrence Collection.

these materials make no mention of their condition at the time of purchase, but in the case of "The First Lady Chatterley," John Kirkpatrick, curator of the Center's Manuscript Department, noticed that the operation of opening and closing the bound manuscript had markedly loosened the sewing thread over the past ten years, creating what were sizeable holes in the paper where the thread entered and exited the paper along the spine folds of the textblock. Also, along the spine of the textblock, the animal glue used to consolidate the gatherings had embrittled enough to introduce stress on the manuscript pages as they were turned. The covering material at the spine of the case was completely detached from the textblock and pressure sensitive adhesive (Scotch) tape was the only material holding the spine fragments to the boards. Thus, both the poor physical condition of the bound manuscript and its relatively frequent use by scholars working at the Center prompted the curator of manuscripts to designate "The First Lady Chatterley" manuscript as a high priority item for conservation treatment.

Because the binding structure of "The First Lady Chatterley" was essentially nonfunctional and was in fact harmful to the textblock, the Conservation Department, in conjunction with the curator, determined that the first version of Lawrence's novel should be removed from its binding and resewn. However, since the binding of the manuscript might have historical significance, the provenance of the manuscript had to be researched and taken into consideration when deciding whether to rebind the manuscript in its extant cover or to make for it a new conservation binding. On initial examination of the Lawrence manuscript, I noticed that the textblock had been rounded and backed and that writing extended up past the shoulder of the textblock to the spine fold. This indicated that the manuscript had been written before the rounding and backing—in short, prior to binding. The fact that there were two different sizes of gatherings comprising the textblock also provided evidence that the manuscript had been written before it had been bound in its current form. Did Lawrence bind the manuscript or have someone bind it for him? If the latter, what was the relationship to Lawrence of the individual who bound the manuscript? If the binding proved to be historically connected to the author, this would argue in favor of reconsolidating the extant binding rather than replacing it with a new conservation binding.

In a letter to "Pino" G. Orioli, Lawrence's Florentine publisher, the author writes: "Suddenly I have the bright idea that the first version of Lady C. may be the right one for Knopf and Seckert. I believe it had hardly any . . . or . . . and no address to the . . .; in fact hardly any of the root of the matter at all. You remember the first version is the one you had bound for Frieda and it is in your flat."[4] Since this passage reveals that upon completion of the manuscript

---

[4]Aldous Huxley, ed., *The Letters of D.H. Lawrence* (London: William Heinemann Ltd., 1932), pp. 810-811.

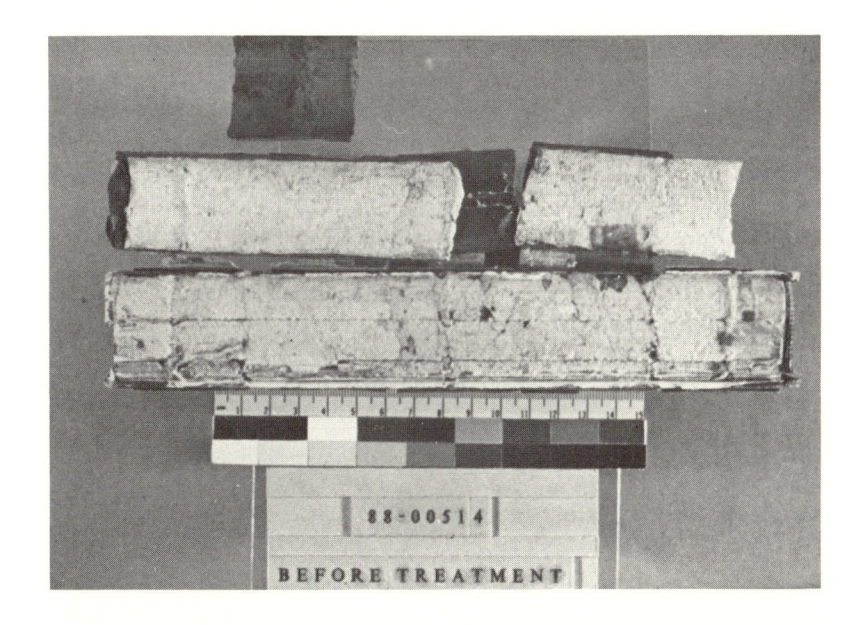

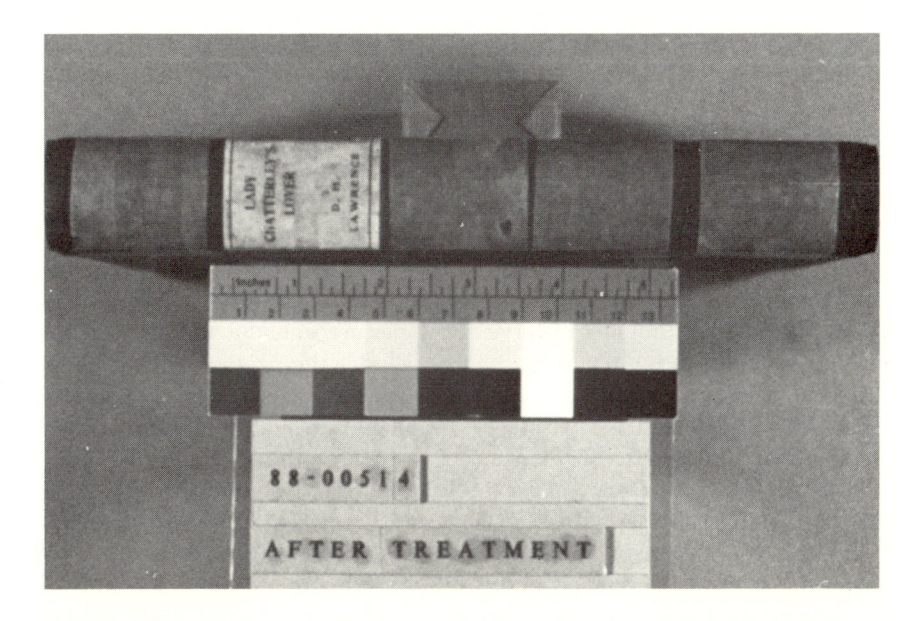

Fig. 1 (above): The spine of the Lawrence manuscript prior to conservation treatment. The sewing, the spine case, and the case-to-text attachment had all broken down. Fig. 2 (below): The spine of the Lawrence manuscript after conservation treatment, including resewing, case-to-text attachment, and reconsolidation of the spinepiece.

Lawrence had sent it to his friend and publisher to be bound for Frieda Lawrence, the binding of "The First Lady Chatterley" manuscript is entwined historically with the author himself. In light of this relationship between the extant binding and the manuscript textblock, the decision was made to rebind the Lawrence manuscript in its extant boards, although the existing sewing pattern and the existing case-to-textblock attachment would need to be redesigned in order to reattach the extant case boards.

After initial examination of the structure and condition of the materials comprising the Lawrence manuscript, a comprehensive conservation treatment proposal was drawn up and submitted to the curator of manuscripts for final approval. Although the tasks of disbinding, mending, and guarding the manuscript would be delicate operations, they were routine treatments not requiring any new structural designs. However, methods of resewing, textblock reconsolidation, and case-to-textblock attachment would require more careful consideration, since new materials would be necessary to rebind the Lawrence manuscript in the extant case boards and new structural designs would be necessary to accomplish the rebinding. The two structural alterations—a new sewing pattern and a new case-to-textblock attachment—would render the artifact structurally self-supporting and would eliminate the damaging effects caused by the extant structure during routine use over the years. Even though the treatment steps to be followed were those for a fairly typical conservation treatment of a unique, casebound book with detached boards, close attention would be paid to the extant materials of the bound manuscript in order to protect those which were inherently more susceptible to damage (i.e., more so than are materials in a printed book) and those already in poor condition.

It is important to examine the materials of which a twentieth-century manuscript is comprised in order to ascertain their longevity in terms of permanence (chemical stability) and durability (physical strength). The conservator must initially observe the structure and the condition of the binding as well as the textblock, which includes the paper, the manuscript ink, the author's collation (if any), the sewing pattern, and the case-to-textblock attachment. Only after examining each of these materials and structures is it possible to determine the most appropriate conservation treatment. The information garnered from examination indicates which materials may be preserved and which must be replaced with appropriate new materials. Reconstruction of the artifact is then carried out with both original materials and with permanent and durable new materials where necessary.

The decision to reformat a manuscript written on paper depends in large part on the longevity of its paper support, and to identify the type and potential permanence of the paper in "The First Lady Chatterley" required a fiber analysis. Disbinding of the textblock unavoidably supplied some paper fragments that could be macerated and used for this purpose. Following the standard procedure as suggested by the Technical Association of the Pulp and Paper Industry, the paper sample was cleansed with a solution of alkali, and then by one of acid, to eliminate additives that could interfere with observation of the paper fiber.[5] Once the paper fragments were transferred to microscope slides and were prepared with a Graff C stain, the fiber analysis was conducted using a Leitz Ortholux II transmitted light microscope, at a magnification of 160x. A fiber morphology and a Graff color chart were then used to determine the type of fiber. From a combination of factors, which included the color the Graff C stain turned when in contact with the paper fibers and the particular morphological features of the fibers, the paper of the Lawrence manuscript was determined to be made from esparto grass.

Esparto is a wiry grass that grows wild in Spain and North Africa, and its use as a papermaking fiber in England arose from the early- and mid-nineteenth-century shortage of papermaking fibers.[6] In the search for chemical methods of treating new papermaking plant fibers, Thomas Routledge developed a soda pulping process for esparto grass that laid the foundation for the esparto papermaking industry first in the United Kingdom and later in France and elsewhere in Europe. In the United States, because of the availability of cheap wood pulp, esparto was never used in the same quantities in papermaking as it was in Europe.[7] During World War II, Europe was cut off from the supply of esparto and the industry never fully recovered. The fact that the manuscript paper of "The First Lady Chatterley" is esparto indicates that historically between the wars, when Lawrence was in Europe and writing this first version of the novel, esparto-based writing paper was still available.

The primary esparto fiber is thin and straight, with long tapering ends and with striations running completely through the fiber. In addition, secondary, associated cells in esparto grass are found in unique configurations that are easily identifiable. During the production of esparto pulp, many of the secondary, associated cells are eliminated, mainly through washing to remove alkali and bleaching materials. However, the two types of associated cells which are normally present in the completed paper are the coarse serrated epidermal cells and the small, comma-shaped seed hairs called trichomes.[8] (See figure 3.) Since both of these types of secondary, associated cells were discovered in large quantities in all the fiber samples of the Lawrence manuscript, this too indicated that the manuscript paper was derived from esparto grass fiber, which is a more permanent (chemically stable) papermaking fiber than twentieth-century writing paper derived from wood fibers.

[5]Sue Beauman Murphy and Siegfried Rempel, "A Study of the Quality of Japanese Papers Used in Conservation," *The Book and Paper Group Annual of the AIC* 4 (1985): 64-65.

[6]Thomas Collings and Derek Milner, "The Identification of Non-Wood Papermaking Fibers: Part 3," *The Paper Conservator* 7 (1982/83): 25.

[7]Ibid.

[8]Ibid.

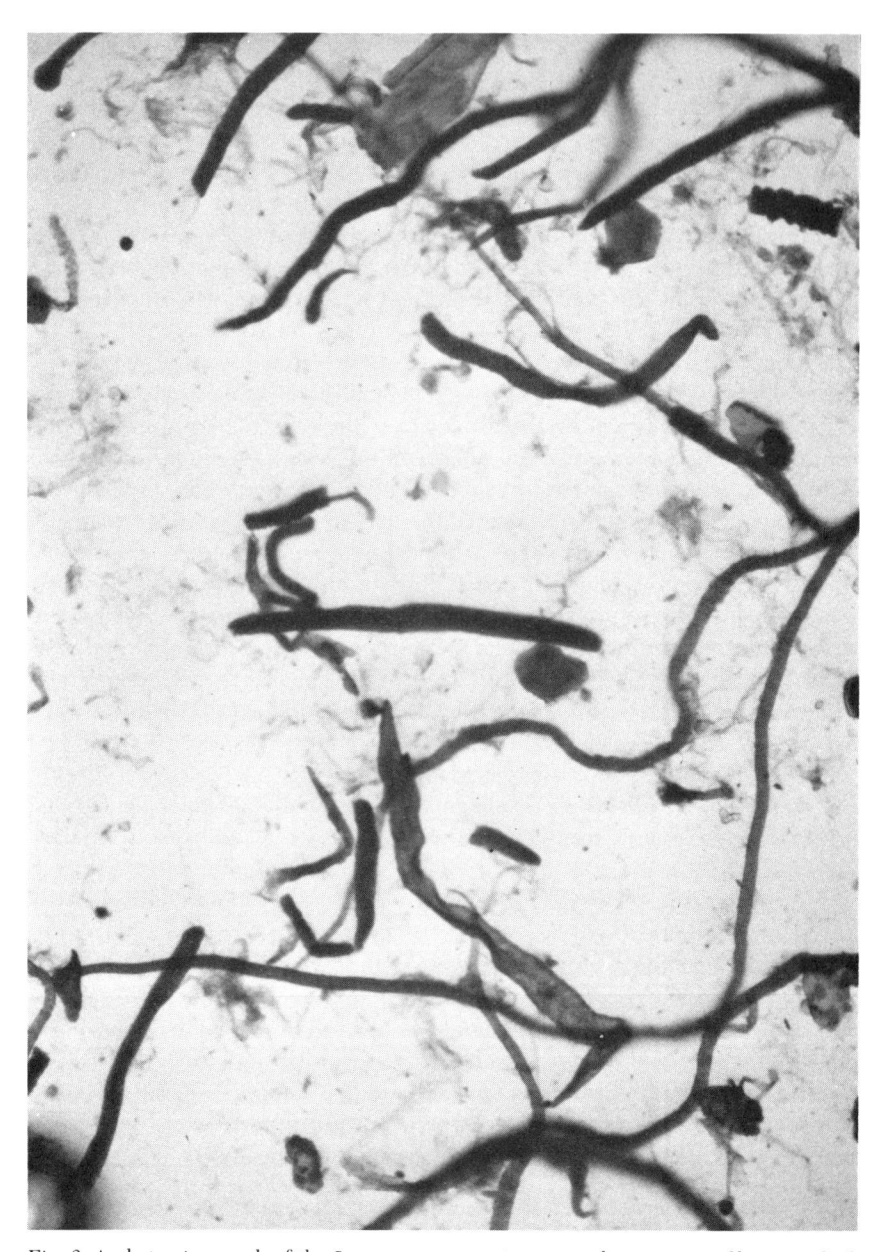

Fig. 3: A photomicrograph of the Lawrence manuscript paper shows esparto fibers at a high magnification. In the upper right quadrant there is a caterpillar-shaped object, which is a serrated epidermal cell characteristically found in samples of esparto paper pulp. Another characteristic cell of esparto pulp is the comma-shaped cell known as a trichome, seen in the upper left quadrant of the sample. Both types of cell matter indicated that the Lawrence manuscript paper was made of esparto fiber.

Even though esparto paper is considered less durable (physical strength) than hardwood paper, it appears to paper chemists to be more permanent (chemically stable) than hardwood paper.[9] Grass pulp such as esparto grass contains fewer ligneous elements initially, which results in less lignin in the final paper product, whereas hardwood pulp derived from wood fiber retains a high degree of lignin, which is a chemically reactive set of compounds known by paper chemists to introduce acidity into paper products. Because the Lawrence manuscript paper contains less lignin than much twentieth-century paper made of wood fiber, "The First Lady Chatterley" manuscript paper has inherently less potential to deteriorate, and this information aided us in determining whether or not the expense of microfilming this modern manuscript was warranted. The next crucial factor in arriving at a decision regarding microfilming of this modern manuscript concerned the inks used in writing the manuscript.

Twentieth-century manuscripts are generally written with sensitive, dye-based inks, which means that they cannot be subjected to the same conservation treatments as twentieth-century books that are printed with an inert, carbon pigment-based printing ink. Visual examination of the inks on the bound manuscript alone provided enough information about their structure and condition to determine that although Lawrence used more than one ink to write the manuscript, all the inks were dye-based and consequently were sensitive to light and to other environmental conditions. The inks had faded in many places, which was recognizable merely by following one ink for a few pages and watching its variation in color. It was also evident from visual examination that the manuscript inks as well as the blue, pen-ruled lines of the paper were highly soluble in water. Since blotches left by previous water stains indicated that the manuscript paper could not withstand any procedures involving immersion in water, this precluded any aqueous examination or treatment of the textblock, such as surface pH testing, washing, or alkalinization. However, if left untreated, the inks could, as time passed, fade to the point of being illegible. To avoid any chance of losing the manuscript to fading, the decision was made to reformat the manuscript in both the microfilm and permanent paper xerox (Permalife) formats as part of the comprehensive conservation plan.

Disbinding the manuscript involved cutting the sewing thread inside each of the gatherings and then pulling apart each gathering from its neighbor. The gatherings of the disbound manuscript were maintained in the order of the authorial collation by carefully observing the proper sequence of the unpaginated pages but without placing extraneous pencil marks anywhere on the manuscript. In the case of a textblock that is in need of rebinding, the conservator uses the collation (i.e., the order of gatherings and the pagination

[9]James P. Casey, *Pulp and Paper Chemistry and Chemical Technology* (New York: Interscience Publishers, Inc., 1960), p. 413.

in either a book or manuscript) to ensure that the text is rebound in its original order. The "collation," a term borrowed from bibliographic notation in the rare-book world, can indicate how the author or printer organized a text. When a bound modern manuscript does not follow the conventions of a printed book, any authorial collation must be relied upon to retain the original order during conservation treatment. In the absence of a conventional printed book collation or an authorial collation, the conservator sometimes imposes a conservation collation of some type on the manuscript. Lawrence did enough of a collation in his manuscript that additional conservation collation—in pencil in a specified place on each page—proved unnecessary. However, pagination of "The First Lady Chatterley" proved unusual in that a music manuscript appears in pencil upside-down approximately halfway through the text. At first sight, this anomaly in the collation seemed inexplicable, and it was difficult to incorporate such a deviation within the normal sequence of pagination. After consulting reference works on Lawrence's correspondence, I realized that Lawrence had been composing the musical score to a play he had written earlier, entitled "David." In a letter dated 16 October 1926 to Robert Atkins, who was producing "David" in London, Lawrence verifies that he was working on the music score to this play at the time he was writing "The First Lady Chatterley,"[10] which explained the presence of this music manuscript among the first handwritten version of Lawrence's novel.

Although Lawrence paginated the manuscript as he wrote it, he did not always do so consistently, with the result that the number of actual pages of manuscript differs from the number of pages Lawrence indicated in his pagination. In the case of the "David" pages, these are not paginated, nor are the blank sheets following these pages, yet all of these must be accounted for in the collation. To maintain order during the conservation treatment, the entire collation of the Lawrence manuscript was documented and was included in the final treatment report, along with a description of the initial physical condition of the manuscript, the treatment proposal and the treatment procedures, and photodocumentation of the manuscript before and after treatment. (All of this information is available to researchers upon request.)

The case-to-textblock attachment in the Lawrence manuscript was originally comprised of two structural features: first, the three sawn-in cords extending onto the inside of the case boards underneath the pasted down endsheet; and second, the outermost endsheet itself, which was pasted down onto the inside of the case boards. Both of these case-to-textblock attachments had broken down and were entirely nonfunctional. All the cords and pastedowns had become severed from the case at the joints, which left the boards detached. Since it was obvious that the original structure of the case-to-textblock attachment had failed in its function, to repeat this structure in rebinding the manuscript was considered inadvisable.

[10]Sagar, *D.H. Lawrence: A Calendar of His Works*, p. 154.

Pressure-sensitive adhesive (Scotch) tape had been applied horizontally across the spine of the bound manuscript to reattach the boards of the binding. Kraft paper tape also had been used for this purpose. Both of these repair efforts had proved unsuccessful, for even though the pressure-sensitive tape and the Kraft paper tape were still adhered to the spine, the spine itself was in fragments. The extent of the damage to the spine was such that it was impossible to determine whether originally it had been supported by a hollow tube, which can relieve pressure on the spine and allow a book to be opened more freely. Thus, the choice to apply a hollow tube during the rebinding of the Lawrence volume was made as a structural measure rather than as an attempt to reconstruct what may have been an original feature of the binding.

Paper repair included mending of tears with wheat starch paste, either alone or with Tosa Tengujo Japanese paper. If the tear was scarfed (i.e., overlapped itself), then the tear was mended by using only wheat starch paste and molding it back together again. If the tear was straight and did not overlap itself, then a thin piece of Tosa Tengujo Japanese paper was pasted over the tear as a reinforcement. (See figures 4 and 5.) Throughout the operation of paper repair, the wheat starch paste had to be quite dry, since any excess moisture could make the manuscript inks and the pen-ruled lines bleed. After mending, guards were made for the outside of the outermost sheet of each gathering using Kizukishi Japanese paper and for the inside of the innermost sheet of each gathering using Tosa Tengujo Japanese paper. All guards were applied flat and then laid flat between a polyester web and blotter under glass and a weight until dry. The first and last gatherings required a heavier weight of Japanese paper hinge (Sekishu) that extended approximately an inch around the exterior of each gathering. (See figure 7.) Once inserted into the delaminated case boards with the linen tapes, the Sekishu hinge would provide a new case-to-textblock attachment, which was designed to distribute the weight more evenly along the length of the case boards and of the textblock (at the outer and inner joints). Following the paper repair, the unbound manuscript was microfilmed in-house by the Center's Photography Department and the entire manuscript was also xeroxed onto permanent paper stock (Permalife) and Velobound into three 11 x 17-inch volumes.

Binding repair commenced while the textblock was being microfilmed. Before removing the pressure-sensitive adhesive (Scotch) tape that extended horizontally around the case spine and onto the case boards in six places, the cover paper and the label were tested to ensure that only the adhesive and the carrier (or tape) of the pressure-sensitive adhesive were soluble in the chosen organic solvents. In this operation, care was taken that no color from the chocolate brown cover paper nor any ink from the label faded or bled. Under a fume hood, naptha and ethanol were used locally with swabs as well as in baths to remove both the carrier and the adhesive residue. Unfortunately, the stains left on the chocolate brown cover paper by the adhesive tape could not be removed completely. In the case of the Kraft paper tape, this was retained on the binding as an intrinsic part of the artifact.

Next the case boards were delaminated at the spine edge approximately an inch into the boards, and this area was then sanded down to create space for the tapes and the Sekishu hinges that would be inserted. The corners of the case boards, which had become pliable, were then reconsolidated by injecting with a syringe a mixture of PVA (polyvinyl acetate, a cold white adhesive) and wheat starch paste into the exposed edges of all four corners of each board. Further repair to the corners, such as recovering them with new material where the board was exposed, was not undertaken since it was considered a cosmetic rather than a structural repair, and alterations to the artifact were made only when structural repair was necessary. The chocolate brown cover paper was lifted from the case boards approximately three-quarters of an inch to expedite the later operation of inserting a new toned paper spine around the original textblock spine and into the area between the board and the original cover paper.

All fifteen of the textblock gatherings, which resemble examination booklets without their telltale blue covers, have a unique number of folios. In resewing the textblock, the varying thicknesses of these gatherings as well as the overall thickness of the textblock were considered in choosing an appropriate weight of new sewing thread and in choosing the width for new sewing supports, which would be linen cloth tapes. After the unbound textblock was microfilmed and xeroxed, it was resewn on a sewing frame, using 20/3 linen for sewing thread and half-inch wide linen tapes for sewing supports in a linked stitch pattern over the tapes. In order to distribute the three tapes evenly along the spine of the textblock, it was not possible to reuse all the original sewing stations (i.e., the holes where the sewing thread passes in and out of the paper at the spine fold). For this reason, new sewing stations were created for resewing the textblock, but this alteration to the artifact was considered necessary in order to provide the structural support for the reconsolidated binding that was lacking in the extant binding.

Following the sewing, the spine was rounded and lightly backed (i.e., "the backs of the sewn sections or leaves are bent over from the center to the left and right until shoulders are formed against which the boards will fit").[11] Even though rounding and backing are never to be considered standard conservation rebinding procedures, especially when a textblock paper is brittle, this process of shaping a ridge or shoulder on each side of the spine was carried out in the case of the Lawrence manuscript to regain the textblock shoulder that was originally present and to distribute the swell of the spine caused by the

---

[11]Matt T. Roberts and Don Etherington, *Bookbinding and the Conservation of Books* (Washington, D.C.: Library of Congress, 1982), p. 15.

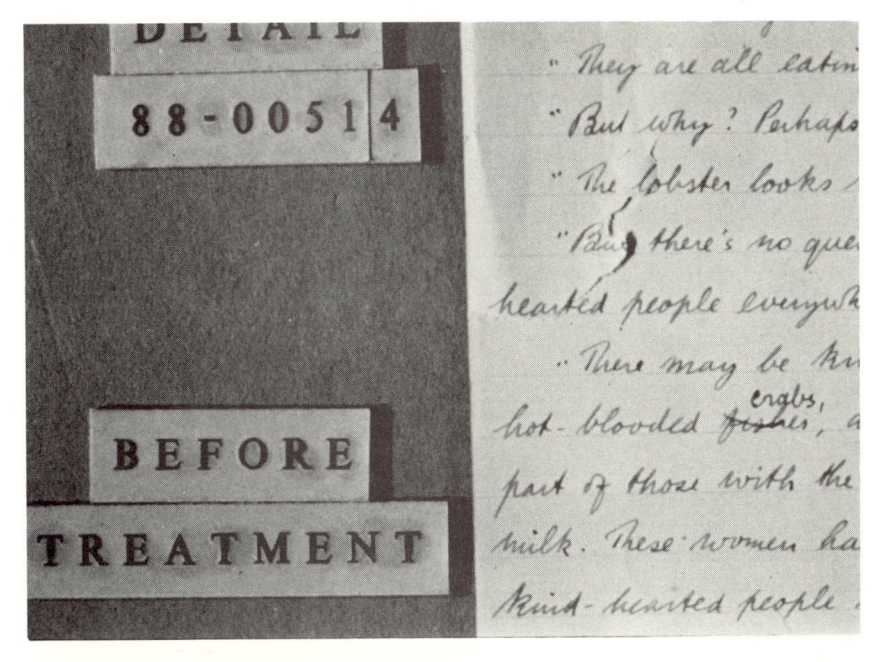

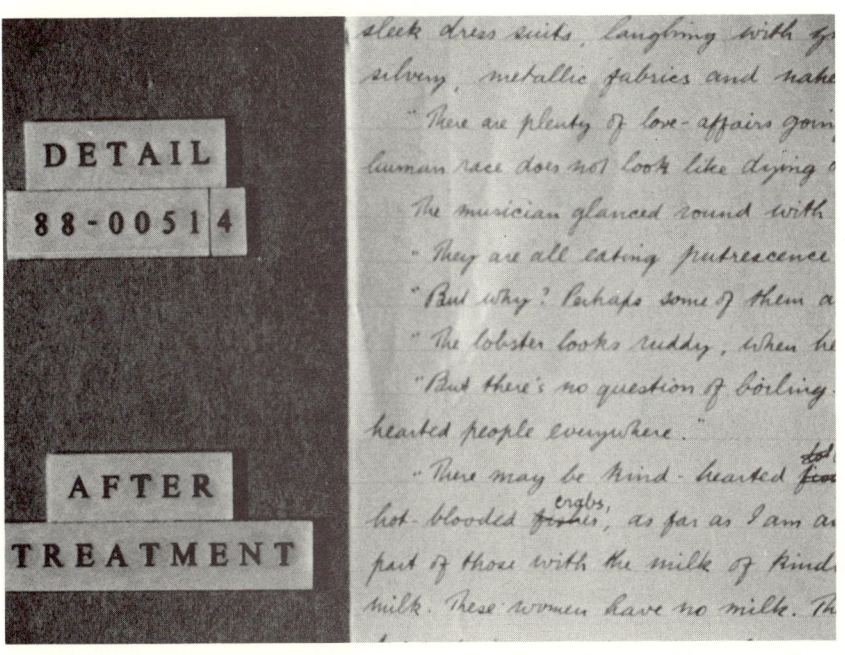

Figs. 4 and 5: This sequence of illustrations shows the detail of a paper tear and its repair, with only wheat starch paste used to mould the tear back together.

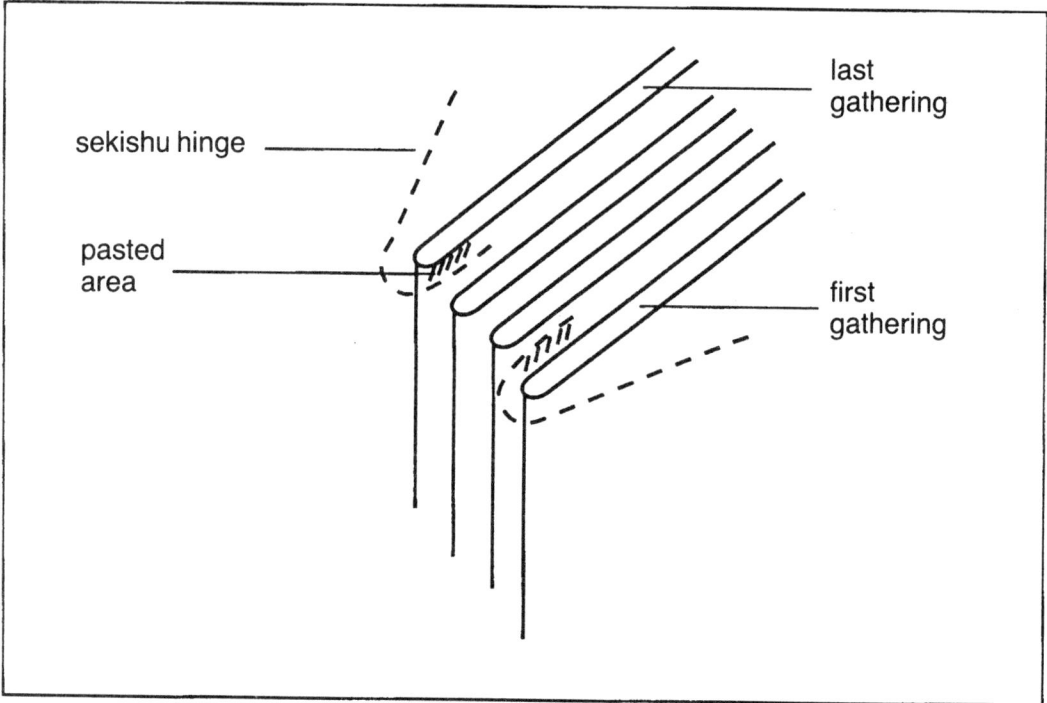

Fig. 6 (above): In resewing the Lawrence textblock, a linked stitch pattern was used with ½" tapes and 20/3 linen thread. Fig. 7 (below): This diagram, rendered by Sharon K. Schmitt, shows the placement of the Sekishu hinges around the first and last gatherings of the Lawrence manuscript.

added bulk of Japanese paper guards on each of the gatherings inside and out. During reconsolidation of the manuscript textblock, the spine was pasted and lined with one layer of Kizukishi Japanese paper between the sewing supports, and two layers of Kizukishi were laid over the entire length of the spine using wheat starch paste. The original headband—there was no tailband—was sewn to linen and readhered with wheat starch paste. A final linen lining (airplane weight) was then applied along the entire length of the spine, also using wheat starch paste. After the linings dried, a hollow tube made of 80 pound Permalife was placed along the spine with a mixture of PVA and wheat starch paste, adhering the paper to the spine, then folding and adhering the paper over itself on each side of the spine to form the hollow, with the excess paper then trimmed away from one side.

The case boards were attached by inserting the tapes and the Sekishu Japanese paper hinges into the delaminated edges of the boards, consolidating them with a mixture of PVA and wheat starch paste, which was syringe-injected on both sides of the tapes and the Sekishu hinges. The manuscript, with case boards attached and number zero double-pointed knitting needles inserted unattached in both joints, in order to define more clearly the joint areas, was then pressed overnight under light pressure.

Next, a piece of Powell handmade paper (medium weight) was toned with acrylics to approximately the same color as the chocolate brown cover paper. The toned Powell paper was cut and formed into a new spine piece and was attached to the hollow and inserted into the delaminated area between the case boards and the outer cover paper. Again, this was consolidated with a mixture of PVA and wheat starch paste using a syringe. (This reconstruction step was not considered reversible, because the next time the manuscript should require rebinding, in all likelihood the extant boards and spine pieces will have degraded and embrittled to the point that the manuscript textblock will need to be rebound in a new conservation binding and the extant boards preserved separately in a protective enclosure. On the other hand, the textblock treatment is reversible and the manuscript textblock can be removed from the case, without disturbing the original materials, by severing the tapes and the Sekishu hinges on each side.) The original spine pieces were then scraped and sanded down to the thickness of the chocolate brown cover paper in order to remove the residue from the original spine lining paper. Afterwards, the original spine pieces were applied to the new spine piece with wheat starch paste. To protect the manuscript against future damage, a drop-spine box was constructed into which the volume would fit snugly but from which it could be removed safely at the spine side where the box folds down flat when opened.

Conservation treatments of twentieth-century manuscripts involve challenging and controversial procedures. To most conservators, manuscript materials created in the twentieth century represent impermanence and a

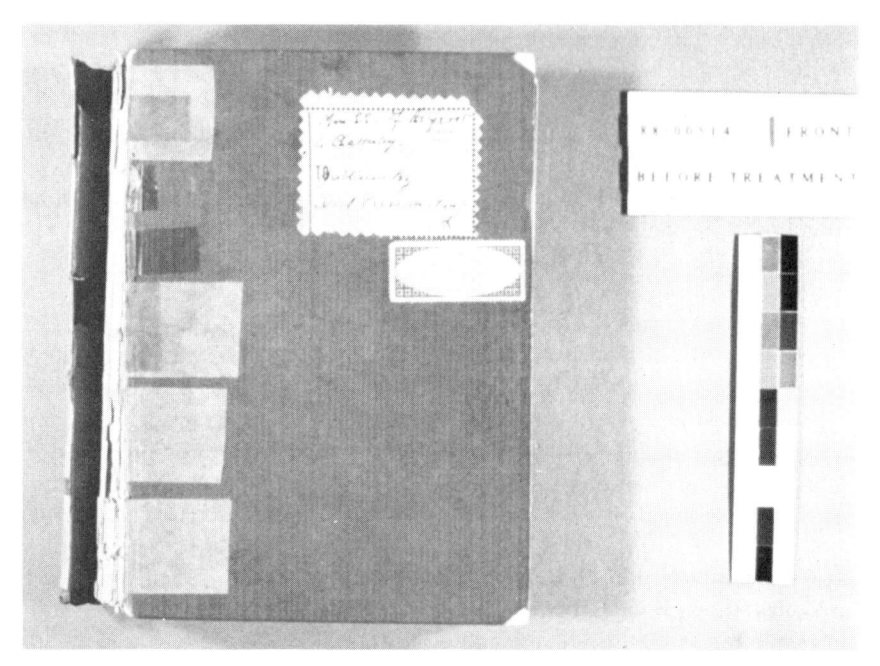

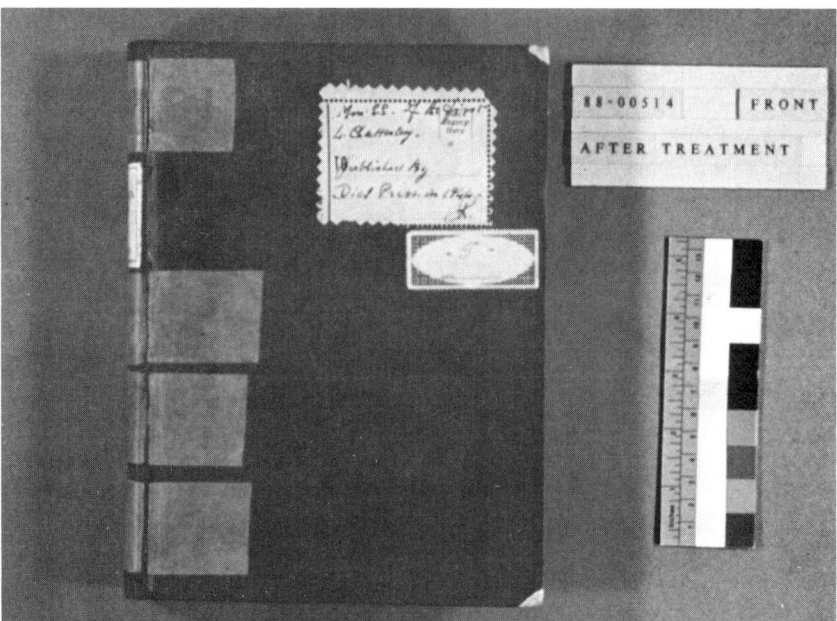

Fig. 8 (above): A front view of the Lawrence manuscript prior to conservation treatment showing the detached front board. Fig. 9 (below): A front view of the Lawrence manuscript after the boards were reattached to the textblock.

lack of durability; consequently, manuscripts of this century which are unique warrant designation as high priority items in the broad conservation and preservation plans of research libraries like the HRHRC. At times such bound modern manuscripts also warrant structural alteration in order to make these twentieth-century works available to the scholarly community. In the conservation treatment of "The First Lady Chatterley" manuscript, the poor overall structure and the poor condition of the materials forced such concessions as the structural alterations to both the sewing pattern and to the case-to-textblock attachment of the extant binding. These structural alterations, if discussed openly and documented fully, will not mislead conservators or scholars of binding history but will protect the manuscript by providing a durable structural support that was lacking in the original binding. The conservation treatment of "The First Lady Chatterley" bound manuscript also reveals the time and effort that goes into researching the materials that comprise such composite twentieth-century artifacts. Because modern manuscripts are often complex and fragile, they require such analytical and historical inquiry into their structures and conditions before the conservator can design a comprehensive conservation treatment proposal.

For a conservator in training, the conservation treatment of this bound manuscript was a fascinating and instructive project. Philosophically, it led to some important discussions and decisions about which periods of modern manuscripts merit priority within the finite conservation and preservation time allotted in the library world of too few conservators. Technically, the project called for new skills in decision making and provided an opportunity to perform a full conservation treatment on a unique artifact. Exemplified in the conservation treatment of "The First Lady Chatterley" bound manuscript was the commitment to thorough documentation, which is consistently carried out by the staff of the HRHRC. Although the D.H. Lawrence Manuscript Collection—owing to its inherent conditions, formats, and patterns of use—will continue to receive conservation care in the future, treatment of "The First Lady Chatterley" was, I believe, a successful solution to a specific twentieth-century conservation problem that was arrived at through cooperation between the Center's paper and book conservators and its curators for manuscripts and historical bindings.

William Faulkner, ca. 11 December 1954, photographed by Carl Van Vechten. *HRHRC Photography Collection*. Reproduced with the permission of the Estate of Carl Van Vechten, Joseph Solomon executor.

Conservation of the Burned Fragments in the William Faulkner Collection

BY ELLEN WEIR

Within the area of manuscript conservation, an unusual problem involves the treatment and preservation of text that was acquired in severely damaged format. Although such cases are not common among the collections of the Harry Ransom Humanities Research Center, the burned poetry manuscripts in the Center's William Faulkner archive represent original, unique, and often unpublished materials that must undergo conservation treatment before they can be safely made available for study. Unlike his later prose work, much of Faulkner's early writing was in verse form and is of increasing significance to those scholars concerned with the development of, and influences on, the art of this major twentieth-century writer.[1] Of the known versions of Faulkner's early verses that are available in public institutions, many at the HRHRC, at The University of Mississippi, and at Southeast Missouri State University consist of fragments that were seriously damaged by fire in 1942.[2] At that time, many of the surviving leaves of early poems were still in the possession of Phil

---

[1] The central study of Faulkner's poetic apprenticeship is Judith L. Sensibar's *The Origins of Faulkner's Art* (Austin: University of Texas Press, 1984). Her *Faulkner's Poetry: A Bibliographical Guide to Texts and Criticism* (Ann Arbor, Michigan: UMI Research Press, 1988) provides a comprehensive listing of all known Faulkner poetry to date. As a young author, Faulkner revised and rewrote his poems many times, and often resubmitted them for publication with minor changes or merely with new titles. Although some of this work was incorporated into handbound volumes that were often handlettered and illustrated by the author for his friends and acquaintances, even these sets underwent later rearrangements and retitling. Of the few surviving examples of these bound texts, the HRHRC collections contain two booklets, both of which are copies of *The Marionettes*, and typescript and manuscript versions of many poems from Faulkner's *Vision in Spring* (1921). See Judith L. Sensibar, Introduction to William Faulkner's *Vision in Spring* (Austin: University of Texas Press, 1984).

[2] Keen Butterworth, "A Census of Manuscripts and Typescripts of William Faulkner Poetry," *Mississippi Quarterly* 26 (Summer 1973): 333. Of the burned fragments, the University of Mississippi Library contains 46 leaves (2 written on both sides); the L.D. Brodsky Collection at Southeast Missouri State University holds 10 leaves; and Yale University has 3 leaves that were given to the institution in 1947. None of the Faulkner poetry in the Berg Collection at the New York Public Library, in the Alderman Library at the University of Virginia, or in the Wisdom Collection at Tulane University is fire-damaged.

Stone, a longtime friend and patron who paid for the printing of *The Marble Faun* (1924), a collection of Faulkner's poetry and his first published book.[3] In 1959, the HRHRC acquired by far the majority of the burned fragments of Faulkner's poetry.

The poetry fragments at the HRHRC present a number of difficulties for Faulkner scholars. The size of the collection, approximately 287 leaves, requires many scholarly and library hours in order to compare the typed and manuscript texts with known printed versions of the poems. Not only have the burned fragments been subjected to frequent handling for purposes of identification but this whole process has been hampered by the fact that some of the text on the surviving leaves was either entirely lost to fire or was made less visible because of damage to the paper. The vulnerable condition of the collection has in turn posed problems for curators and conservators, since increased interest in the burned fragments has created the danger of further damage to their already fragile state. In an effort to safeguard the collection and yet make the poetry accessible to scholars, the curator of the manuscript collection placed the Faulkner burned fragments on a priority list for conservation treatment. It is the double goal of the Conservation Department to stabilize these fragments so that they will not deteriorate, or will do so less rapidly, and to house the documents in such a way as to make them available to the scholar while minimizing the risk to their continued existence.

Among the Center's collection of Faulkner manuscript poems and poem fragments (mostly typescripts) are versions of verses included in his hand-bound sequence, *Vision in Spring*, presented by the author in 1921 to his future wife, Estelle Franklin. Subsequently, what may have been a revision of this poem sequence was submitted in 1923 for publication as *Orpheus, and Other Poems*. Even though the manuscript of *Orpheus* is now lost, versions of poems from this collection may be among the burned fragments at the HRHRC.[4] Other individual poems and collections represented in the Center's holdings include an early typescript of *The Marble Faun* (published in 1924 by The Four Seas Co.); the setting copy and galley proofs for *A Green Bough* (published in 1933 by Smith and Haas); two of the four known extant handbound copies of *The Marionettes* (1920); holograph drafts of "Love Song," Faulkner's parody of T.S. Eliot's "J. Alfred Prufrock"; numerous still unpublished lyrics; early drafts of poems Faulkner later included in a sequence of love sonnets he gave to Helen Baird in 1926 (*Helen: A Courtship*); and "Estelle." Since their acquisition by the HRHRC, many of the burned

---

[3]James W. Webb and A. Wigfall Green, eds., *William Faulkner of Oxford* (Baton Rouge: Louisiana State University Press, 1965), p. 4.

[4]Sensibar, *Vision*, pp. x-xi. *Orpheus, and Other Poems* may have been the first full-length manuscript Faulkner ever submitted to a publisher, in this case The Four Seas Company of Boston. For more information on this manuscript, see Joseph Blotner, *Faulkner, A Biography* (New York: Random House, 1974), pp. 347, 349-50.

fragments have been recognized by various scholars as early versions of the printed poems, but there are still a large number of fragments that have yet to be identified. If the text of a fragment remains unidentified, it has been catalogued by the Center under the first complete or first visible line. In some cases, as the leaves have undergone conservation treatment, fragments previously catalogued as separate items have been found to join together. Once they have been treated and reattached, these fragments will be recatalogued as one item under their proper title.

THE BURNED FRAGMENTS

The types of paper, the shape of the fragment, and the inks used may all offer clues that will aid in the scholarly identification of the manuscripts. Present in the collection are various types of paper, including lightweight "Bond" stationery, inexpensive writing paper, and "onion skin" typing paper. All leaves suffered some degree of damage from the fire, and in most cases the remaining fragments are approximately two-thirds to three-fourths the size of the original sheet, while some are only one-eighth the original size. Several recurrent shapes to the fragments suggest that they were in piles or in groups at the time of the fire. Most of the 287 leaves are typed in blue, black, or violet typing ink or are typed carbon copies. Some bear notations in pencil or in writing ink; most have text on the recto (front) only. A number of typed leaves show the poet's holograph (not necessarily of the typed poem or recto) on the opposite side (verso), and there is one typed leaf on which Faulkner drew an illustration in a bluish-green writing ink.

As a result of the fire, the papers have darkened considerably and exhibit browned, charred, and very brittle edges that easily break with handling. Generally, the papers are also very dry and fragile, again as a result of their exposure to heat. Many of the leaves display an oily residue that probably exuded from the paper and that remains as a byproduct of an incomplete combustion. Many leaves also have soot, ash, and carbonized flakes on their surfaces, and many bear tide marks (stains left from drops or pools of water) as well as evidence of mold growth (inactive mold spores, multi-colored stains, and abrasion of the surface of the paper due to the activity of the mold).

At an unknown point in the history of these leaves, several different attempts were made, somewhat unsatisfactorily, to conserve approximately twenty of the fragments. Some of these were "silked," a process used extensively since the beginning of the twentieth century in which a layer of finely woven silk fabric is placed on one or both sides of a document and adhered with paste in order to provide the sheet with a layer of support to increase its handleability. Several of the leaves were laminated with a cellulose acetate tissue, also in an effort to reinforce the brittle fragments.

While these procedures had achieved their immediate aim of increasing handleability, they also had resulted in further discoloration and partial obscuring of the texts.

TWENTIETH-CENTURY PAPER

All the fragments in the Faulkner collection of burned manuscripts are on twentieth-century paper made from wood pulp, which creates special problems for conservators. Paper is made from a wide variety of plant fibers of varying lengths and sizes, bonded together to form a fibrous web, or sheet. The length and strength of the fibers contribute greatly to the strength of the finished product, with longer fibers forming a stronger and more durable paper. Most chemists believe that all plant fibers contain cellulose, which comprises the cell basis of the fibers, and lignins, which are the acid-producing gum and resin polymers that can accelerate a paper's rate of acidic degradation. When paper is manufactured, the lignins are processed out of the fibers as much as possible by chemical and mechanical means.[5]

Until the mid-nineteenth century, most Western papers were made from cotton or linen fibers, but as the demand for paper increased and new technology was developed, wood pulp became a cheap and readily available substitute for cotton and linen rags. Wood fibers generally have a higher lignin content than other plant fibers, so that for purposes of papermaking, chemical and/or mechanical processing of wood fibers attempts to eliminate as much lignin as possible. Nonetheless, higher lignin content in wood fibers and the effects of the complex procedures for processing—such as the addition of chemicals to the pulp and/or the grinding of fibers—together produce a paper that deteriorates at a much faster rate than a paper made of other fibers. In combination with such twentieth-century factors as artificial light and air pollution, as well as the effects of sizings and bleaches introduced into the pulp, the lignin content and the chemical additives result in a paper with a comparatively short life expectancy. One of the major goals of conservation treatment is to attempt to neutralize the acids in the paper so that its inevitable deterioration can be slowed.

---

[5]Roy P. Whitney, "Chemistry of Paper," in *Paper–Art and Technology*, ed. Paulette Leny and Robert Leveing (San Francisco: World Print Council, 1979), pp. 36-38.

Fig. 1: Before treatment: carbon copy typescript fragment from the poem "Eunice." The two pieces seen here were previously catalogued separately. During documentation, in preparation for treatment, it was discovered that the two fragments joined; they were later reattached. See fig. 10, p. 76.

DOCUMENTATION

After manuscripts are chosen for conservation treatment by the curator, they are thoroughly documented by the Conservation Department before treatment begins. The leaves are photographed, photocopied (when it is determined that this procedure will not damage the item), and documented on a treatment report form. The physical characteristics and the condition of the item are described in detail, with diagrams drawn at times to illustrate characteristics that may not be apparent in a photograph or a photocopy. A treatment strategy is then decided upon and a written proposal is given to the curator for his review, comments, approval, and signature. Included in this treatment proposal are the conservator's comments on the possible effects of treatment. In this way, the curator is advised if a treatment could possibly alter the physical characteristics of an artifact, such as changing the color of the paper or diluting the ink. The curator may then make an informed decision, balancing the benefits of conservation treatment against any possible loss of scholarly information. All procedures performed on the items are carefully noted on the treatment report form, and comments are recorded as to the results of treatment. In this way, conservators are creating a written history of the object before and after conservation, which is then made available to the curator or patron.

Because of the varied and unusual conditions of the Faulkner burned fragments, development of a treatment strategy involved a fairly complex set of issues. The concerns raised by poor paper quality, soot, surface soil, mold damage, water damage, fragility of the paper, residual deposits, and the ill effects of prior treatment all had to be addressed. The treatment approach that was settled upon deals with these major categories, at the same time that it allows for the individual conditions of each leaf.

TREATMENT PROPOSAL

Before proceeding with treatment of the Faulkner burned manuscripts, the following steps of a proposed strategy were submitted to the curator. First, the conservators would brush off carefully from the fragment any loose deposits of soil and soot. Next, the fragment would be bathed in distilled water, a procedure that is often used to reintroduce moisture to the sheet and to remove from the paper soil and cellulose-damaging acids and byproducts of deteriorated cellulose. Cellulose and its byproducts tend to diffuse in a water bath, thus raising the pH of the paper from the acidic range to a more neutral and stable level. (pH, a measure of the concentration of hydrogen ions, indicates the level of acidity vs. alkalinity within a substance and is measured on a logarithmic scale of 0 [most acidic] to 14 [most alkaline], with a measurement of 7 being neutral. Ideally, paper should be neutral or slightly alkaline to obtain optimum longevity. In applying this measurement to the burned fragments, the pH is monitored as an indicator of the level of damaging acids in the paper. As manuscript treatment is performed, the numerical measurement of a leaf may increase, indicating that to some degree the acids are in fact being neutralized.)[6] In an attempt to eliminate other such byproducts, the fragments would be bathed subsequently in distilled water and in a very small amount of ammonium hydroxide. The use of ammonium hydroxide both raises the pH level of the bath solution and helps to remove more acids by acting as a swelling and cleansing agent. Also, the fragment could be bathed in a solvent, such as ethyl alcohol, in order to reduce or eliminate compounds of soot and oily residue on the surface of the paper. If appropriate, the fragment would then be immersed in an alkaline solution of distilled water and calcium hydroxide or magnesium bicarbonate to increase the pH and introduce an alkaline reserve into the paper as a buffer to inhibit further acidic degradation.

The next step would be to coat the fragments with hydroxypropyl cellulose, a commercially prepared powdered cellulose manufactured under the trade name Klucel G ("G" representing a measure of viscosity). Klucel G can be suspended in various solvents to form a gel, and when applied to fragile paper, the gel is absorbed into the sheet, adding to and reinforcing the cellulose structure, which essentially reduces the brittleness of the paper and appears to give plasticity to the sheet. At this point, the tears, fractures, and separated pieces of the fragments would be realigned to their appropriate positions and the sheet then lined with L-tissue (a very thin semi-transparent paper) adhered with a wheat-starch paste. This backing would be applied to the verso of the leaf, providing there was no text present on the back of the fragment, and would serve to mend the sheet while lending it added support. The excess lining tissue would be trimmed away and the lined fragment encapsulated in a protective covering or sleeve made from polyester film, which would be sealed to hold the fragment in position.

Since earlier treatments have generally been considered detrimental to the items in the Faulkner collection of burned fragments, it was decided that the previous treatment should be "reversed," that is, to remove the silks and laminates introduced in the past. Because the history of the silking and lamination of these fragments is unknown, it could not be determined whether or not the twenty leaves treated previously had undergone the above steps for reducing their acidity levels. For this reason, once the silking and

---

[6]For a discussion of pH, see *Science For Conservators*, Book 2–*Cleaning* (London: Crafts Council, 1983), pp. 90-103.

lamination processes had been reversed, the fragments would be subjected to the same treatment procedures as the rest of the collection.

Although there are similarities in paper and media, each leaf would need to be evaluated individually on the basis of its particular combination of media and paper characteristics. The inks would be carefully tested for their solubility in water and in other solvents that might be considered for use in treatment. For instance, an ink that "offset" when tested by contact with a damp blotter would lead the conservator to reconsider washing the item in water, to abandon entirely this procedure and consider another approach, or to proceed with the washing while taking care to monitor the treatment in order to minimize the possible diffusion of the ink into the bath water.

Fig. 2: Detail of "silked" fragment (unidentified text).

Reversing Previous Treatments

Once the curator of the manuscript collection had approved the treatment proposal, the first step was to reverse the silking and lamination processes. Silking is still a procedure used today as a conservation measure in some cases, but it has largely been judged unsatisfactory and has been abandoned by many conservators because of the effects to the paper over time.[7] As a natural protein, silk is subject to deterioration from acids, and after exposure to acids it tends with age to discolor and eventually to disintegrate. The paste layer applied to the manuscript in attaching the silk support must be fairly thick in order to hold the silk in place, and since paste may contain impure products, this too can discolor the paper, especially when applied improperly.

In the case of the burned fragments, the silk had become brittle and had begun to deteriorate. Also, the paper exhibited the detrimental effects (darkening and discoloration) of the starch paste with which the silk was adhered. Placing a silked leaf in a molded fiberglass tray filled with distilled water, the paste was softened so that the silk could be removed. After about thirty minutes, the leaf was taken from the bath and placed on a light table (of clear plexiglass illuminated from beneath to allow for better visibility) and the silk was easily peeled away from the paper fragment. The leaf was then immersed in another bath containing distilled water and an enzyme that hastened the dissolution of the paste layer. This amylase enzyme (a natural, starch-digesting protein) rapidly breaks down starch adhesives and eliminates the need to remove the paste manually (usually by scraping) from areas that are particularly sensitive to this abrasive technique (such as over the typed or handwritten text).[8] After a short time in this solution, the fragment was removed and allowed to dry on a drying rack.

Several of the leaves had been laminated with a cellulose acetate tissue. In this process, a sheet of thin paper with heat-activated plastic coating made from cellulose acetate is placed on either side of the document. This package is then placed in a heated press that softens the cellulose acetate adhesive and is passed through rollers under heavy pressure, resulting in a fairly stiff but handleable sheet of paper.[9] The problem with using this procedure for the Faulkner collection of burned fragments was that the text had been partially obscured or dulled by the opaque appearance of the laminate tissue. Also, the laminate made the flexibility, texture, and tactile nature of the paper inaccessible to study by researchers.

---

[7] W.J. Barrow, *Manuscripts and Documents: Their Deterioration and Restoration* (Charlottesville: The University Press of Virginia, 1976), p. 66.

[8] Pia C. DeSantis, "Some Observations on the Use of Enzymes in Paper Conservation," *Journal of American Institute of Conservation* 23, no. 1 (Fall 1983): 7.

[9] Chandru J. Shahani and William K. Wilson, "Preservation of Libraries-Archives," *American Scientist* 75 (1987): 240.

To remove the cellulose acetate tissue from the burned fragments, each leaf was immersed in an acetone bath. Acetone, a solvent that breaks down the cellulose acetate impregnated in the tissue layer, softened the acetate in about five minutes and the tissue was then peeled away from the fragment with tweezers. Next, the fragment was turned over in the bath and the other layer of tissue removed. The leaf was then placed in two or three consecutive baths of acetone and ethyl alcohol (another solvent effective in dissolving the cellulose acetate) for about ten minutes per bath, which eliminated the remaining acetate from the paper. Finally, the leaf was removed from the last bath and allowed to air dry. For protection from the toxic fumes of the solvents, the conservator conducts the entire procedure under a fume hood (a large vented cabinet with a stainless steel working surface). Also, the conservator wears latex gloves to prevent absorption of the solvent through the skin.

WASHING IN DISTILLED WATER

At this writing, most of the inks in the fragments tested have not reacted adversely to water and have therefore been good candidates for aqueous treatment. The paper can be safely washed in a tray of water and removed without damage, but each sheet requires very careful and calculated handling. A molded fiberglass tray, approximately 21 x 27 inches, is prepared with the following ingredients: about 1½ inches of distilled water; a piece of plastic grating in the bottom to elevate the fragment for safer handling and to allow sufficient flow of water beneath the leaf; a piece of nylon screening to support the fragment; and a piece of "wet strength" paper to support and cushion the fragment during the bath and to prevent possible impressions from the nylon screening and plastic grating supports. The "wet strength" paper is absorbent and retains its shape and strength even when immersed in solution for long periods of time.

Although the fibers of a sheet of paper remain intact when washed, they tend to swell when wet, causing the paper to curl when it is first moistened. This does not generally present a problem with most sturdy papers, but handling dry and brittle fragments can be particularly perilous. When these fragile fragments are first moistened, usually by spray with a fine mist, the curl can be so dramatic that it threatens to fracture the paper even further. The browned and charred edges are particularly vulnerable to this phenomenon. The rate at which the moisture is applied must therefore be carefully controlled.

In order to relax the fragments before immersing them in the bath, they were first placed on a small piece of "wet strength" paper and sprayed slowly

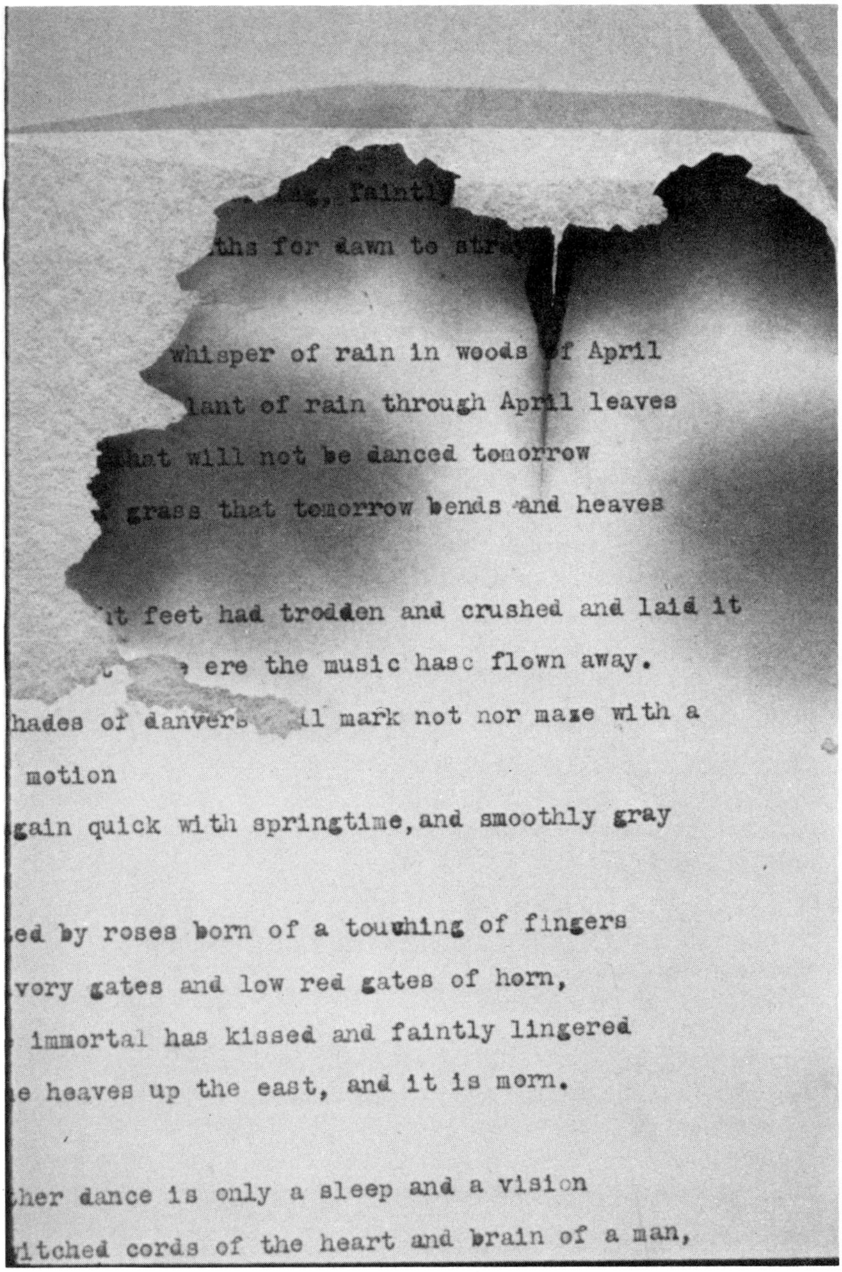

..., faintly
...ths for dawn to stra...

... whisper of rain in woods of April
... lant of rain through April leaves
...at will not be danced tomorrow
... grass that tomorrow bends and heaves

...t feet had trodden and crushed and laid it
... ere the music hasc flown away.
hades of danvers ...il mark not nor maze with a
motion
gain quick with springtime, and smoothly gray

ed by roses born of a touching of fingers
vory gates and low red gates of horn,
 immortal has kissed and faintly lingered
e heaves up the east, and it is morn.

her dance is only a sleep and a vision
itched cords of the heart and brain of a man,

Fig. 3: Same fragment of unidentified text as in fig. 2, with silking removed and backed with lining tissue.

with distilled water, allowing sufficient time between each application of fine mist for it to be absorbed into the paper fibers. Because of their fragility, the fragments could not be turned over to spray the other side and thereby speed up the relaxing process. Once the fragment was sufficiently relaxed, both the paper and its wet strength support were placed on the surface of the water in the tray. After carefully submerging and removing the wet strength paper, the fragment was free to float on the surface tension of the water. The fragment was then sprayed to cover it with pools of water, causing it to sink gently until it came to rest on the wet strength, nylon screening, and plastic grating in the bottom of the tray. The inks were closely observed for any evidence that they were being dissolved by the water, and care was taken not to agitate the fragment in any way while in the bath so that it would not be damaged by colliding into the sides of the tray. The fragment was allowed to remain in the bath for about two hours, at which time the water could become tinged

Fig. 4: Burned fragment from "The Marionettes" during treatment in bath of distilled water.

yellowish brown as the acids and byproducts of the decomposed cellulose were diffused in the bath. The fragment was then lifted from the bath by sliding the supporting nylon screening and wet strength up and out of the tray. All of these layers were then placed on a drying rack to dry thoroughly. In most cases, water stains, tide marks, and overall discoloration had been, to varying degrees, lessened by bathing in distilled water. Also, moisture was reintroduced into the sheets, reducing somewhat the brittle condition of the fragments.

Treatment in Ethyl Alcohol

It was determined through testing that ethyl alcohol was most effective in reducing oily deposits on the surface of the paper. Fragments selected as appropriate for this treatment were immersed individually in a small tray containing enough ethyl alcohol to cover the paper. Each fragment was left in the tray for about thirty minutes and was then removed from the bath and allowed to air dry. This treatment was generally successful in dissolving oily residues and was believed to be effective in rendering the mold spores inactive. However, bathing in ethyl alcohol tends to dry out the fibers of the paper because the solvent evaporates very rapidly, pulling out moisture with it. Therefore, subsequent water baths were helpful in reintroducing moisture into the paper fibers.

Ammonium Hydroxide Baths

Once the ethyl alcohol treatment was concluded, the fragments could then be bathed in a solution of distilled water and a very small amount of ammonium hydroxide. The addition of this chemical compound raised the measurement of the bath water to about a 9.5 to 10.5 pH level, and washing in this slightly alkaline solution removed more acids from the paper, helping it to approach a neutral (7.0) pH measurement. Next, using a Fisher pH meter, the pH was monitored by measuring the surface of the paper. In this operation, the flat end of the meter's sensitive electrode—placed on the surface of the dampened and relaxed paper—measures the activity of the hydrogen ions as they are drawn from the paper onto the dampened surface and translates this activity into a numerical measurement. However, surface measurement is merely an indication of the pH level of the paper and cannot be considered conclusive. Although more sophisticated processes can be performed so that the electrode makes fuller contact with the ions and achieves a more accurate reading of their activity, these methods are not appropriate for this treatment since they would involve the destruction (repulping) of a paper sample. Before any aqueous treatment was performed on the fragments, the pH of the paper measured between 3.8 and 5.0, which was definitely in the acidic range. Bathing in distilled water alone raised the pH to about 4.8 to 5.3. After washing in distilled water and ammonium hydroxide, the surface pH measurement indicated 5.6 to 5.8, which was much nearer the neutral level.

ALKALINIZATION

If, after these two aqueous treatments, the surface pH of the paper was in the measurably acidic range (6.0 and below), and if the media was stable, the fragments were then considered for further baths in a more concentrated alkaline solution of magnesium bicarbonate or calcium hydroxide and distilled water. The higher pH of these baths further neutralized the acids and introduced a buffer of alkaline salts into the paper, which will slow the progression of acidic degradation by absorbing and neutralizing the acids as they continue to attack the paper fibers. This alkalinization step was also desirable because the proposed encapsulation of the fragments in polyester would create a microenvironment in which the activity of the remaining acids in the paper might accelerate. The solution used in the bath was approximately 5 to 6 parts water to 1 part magnesium bicarbonate or calcium hydroxide. In this treatment, the fragments were immersed for approximately 10 minutes each and then allowed to air dry. Magnesium bicarbonate was preferred because it tends not to leave a powdery precipitate on the surface of the paper when dry, as does the calcium hydroxide solution. The charred edges of these leaves are generally very fragile, so that even though gentle brushing of the surface to remove this precipitate is possible without causing damage, any extra manipulation was avoided whenever possible.

KLUCEL G

Next, the surface of the fragments, front and back, were coated with the cellulose derivative Klucel G (hydroxypropyl cellulose), dissolved in ethyl alcohol *or* isopropyl alcohol (depending on the results of the testing of the inks) in a 1% solution. When applied to fragile paper, Klucel G is absorbed into the sheet, adds to and reinforces the cellulose structure, and thus slightly reduces its brittleness and makes it more handleable. The application of the gel also reduces the likelihood of creating or worsening fractures and splits in the paper during its use in the library system. In this treatment, the gel was applied with a soft bristled brush and allowed to dry.

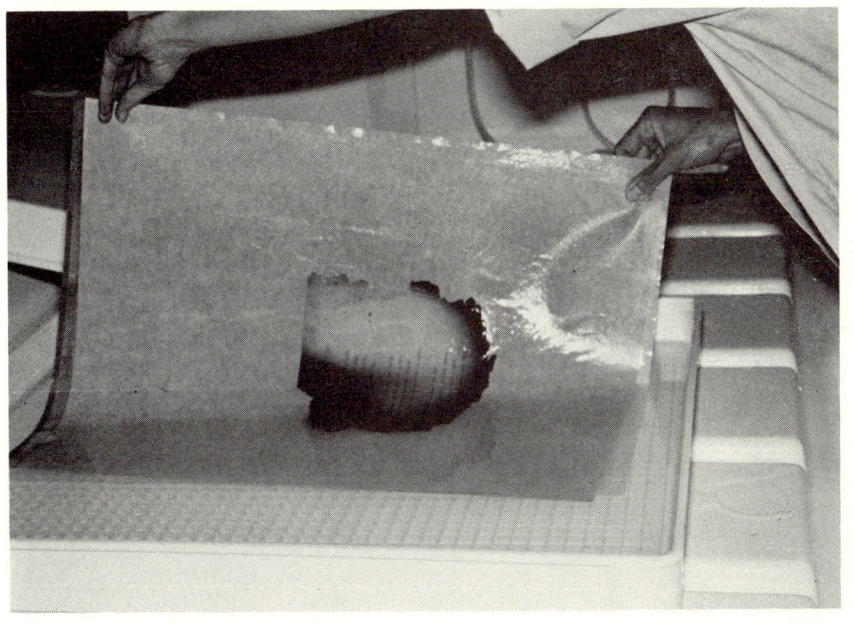

Fig. 5 (above): Another fragment from "Eunice" immersed in ethyl alcohol in a disposable polyester tray. Fig. 6 (below): Fragment clinging to support as it is removed from the bath.

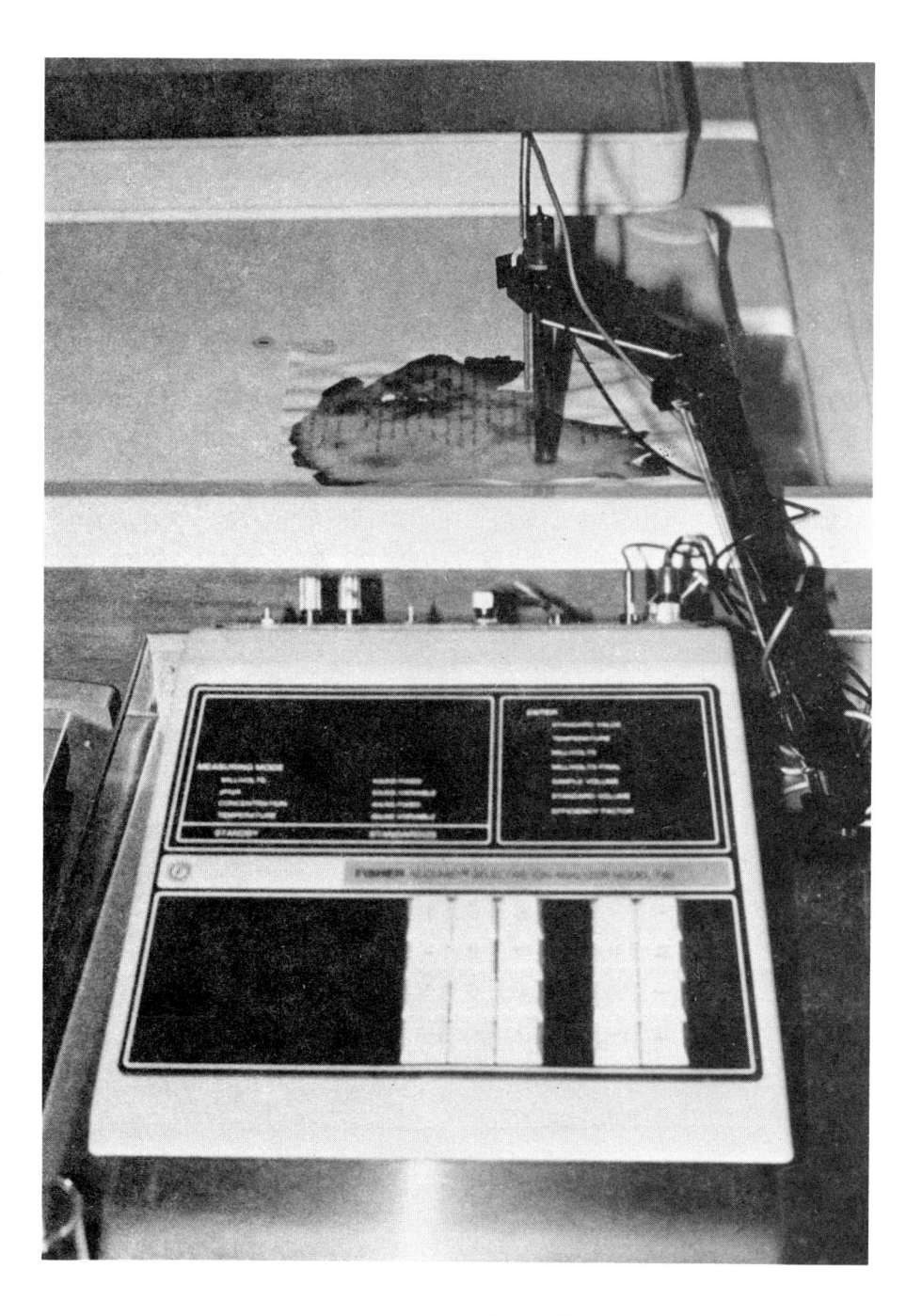

Fig. 7: pH meter taking surface measurement.

Lining

The fragments were now ready to be lined. Pieces of L-tissue (a very thin paper made from bast fibers, which are generally pH neutral) were cut about 3 to 4 inches larger on all sides than the fragments to be lined. Generally, lining is applied to the backs of fragments with text on one side only, so as not to obscure any scholarly information. Those with small amounts of script or typing on their verso may also be lined, but in these cases a "window" is cut out of the lining tissue to accommodate the text. The pieces of lining were then sprayed repeatedly with a fairly concentrated calcium hydroxide solution in an effort to introduce an alkaline buffer into this backing paper. When in contact with (adhered to) a buffered lining paper, the fragment would be more likely to retain its neutral or slightly alkaline nature, perhaps providing the paper with some extra protection against damaging acids.

Next, the recto sides of the fragments were sprayed with distilled water and the paper relaxed slowly, in the same manner as when it was bathed in the tray. A piece of polyester film was then sprayed liberally and this wet surface placed on the dampened fragment. The surface tension of the water on both surfaces allowed the leaf to cling to the polyester film and to be transported safely. This package of fragment and polyester film was then placed on a special light table built into a sink that safely allowed a translucent view of the artifact while undergoing wet treatment. At this time, the back (verso) of the leaf (which is the side to be lined) was facing the conservator. Using the light table, small detached fragments were repositioned and tears and splits realigned, with the water between the relaxed fragments and the polyester film allowing for this type of manipulation. Trapped air pockets were also manipulated out so that the fragments would become perfectly flat. The lining tissue was then ready for application.

For adhering the lining tissue, a wheat-starch paste was prepared in advance. This type of paste is regularly used by paper conservators because it is soluble in water and can therefore be easily removed if necessary. The paste is diluted with distilled water until it is the consistency of light cream. Placing the dry lining tissue on another piece of polyester film, the diluted paste was quickly brushed on with a broad, flat brush until all the wrinkles were smoothed out, the surface was completely flat, and the paste was evenly distributed. The pasted lining tissue, clinging to the polyester film support, was then lifted and carefully positioned on top of the fragment lying on the light table, with the pasted surface of the lining tissue making contact with the verso of the leaf. Slight pressure was then applied to the package in order to aid in the adhesion of the lining, the polyester film was removed from both sides, and the lined fragment was placed between blotters to remove excess moisture. Since it is crucial that the fragment and lining tissue dry as evenly as possible so as to minimize distortion or curling of the paper, blotters were changed frequently, each time placing the package between fresh blotters and under the weight of a marble slab. For several days while drying, the lined fragments were kept between blotters and under weights. The excess lining tissue around the edges of the fragment was then trimmed to roughly rectangular yet aesthetically pleasing dimensions.

ENCAPSULATION

The lined fragments were then protected by encapsulating them individually in polyester film. In this procedure, developed by the Library of Congress, the artifact is sandwiched between two sheets of polyester film and sealed. Testing indicates that polyester film is a durable material that will not deteriorate under normal library conditions. Other advantages to the use of polyester film are: 1) it is an inert material that will not reintroduce acids to the treated manuscript; 2) it has a slight static charge that holds the manuscript in place; and 3) it is impact absorbing and highly flexible, which allows the encapsulated manuscript to be handled and flexed without endangering the item or worsening the inherent condition of its paper.[10] This procedure is also reversible since there is no adhesion of paper to polyester and the film may be cut easily with a scalpel. After inserting the manuscript between the polyester sheets, the film was sealed using an ultrasonic welder, a machine that rearranges the molecular structure of the polyester, causing the two layers to form a bond at a specific location, without the use of adhesives. In this treatment, the welds were positioned as close to the fragment as possible in order to minimize the remote possibility of the fragment shifting within the sleeve and to create a firm, stable bond.

CONCLUSIONS

The treatment of the burned manuscripts from the William Faulkner Collection has presented unique challenges to the Conservation Department. The resulting product is one that can be handled safely and therefore can be made available to the patron. Also, the conserved fragments are easily stored in folders and manuscript boxes in the stacks of the Center. In addition, treatment has slowed the inevitable deterioration of these twentieth-century papers and has provided them with more structural integrity, at the same time that it has reunited previously detached fragments of text, thereby making more of the information readily available for scholarly research. Finally, in

[10]Peter Waters, "An Assessment of Lamination and Encapsulation," *The Conservation of Library and Archive Materials and the Graphic Arts* (Cambridge, 1980): 74.

WASHINGTONIANA

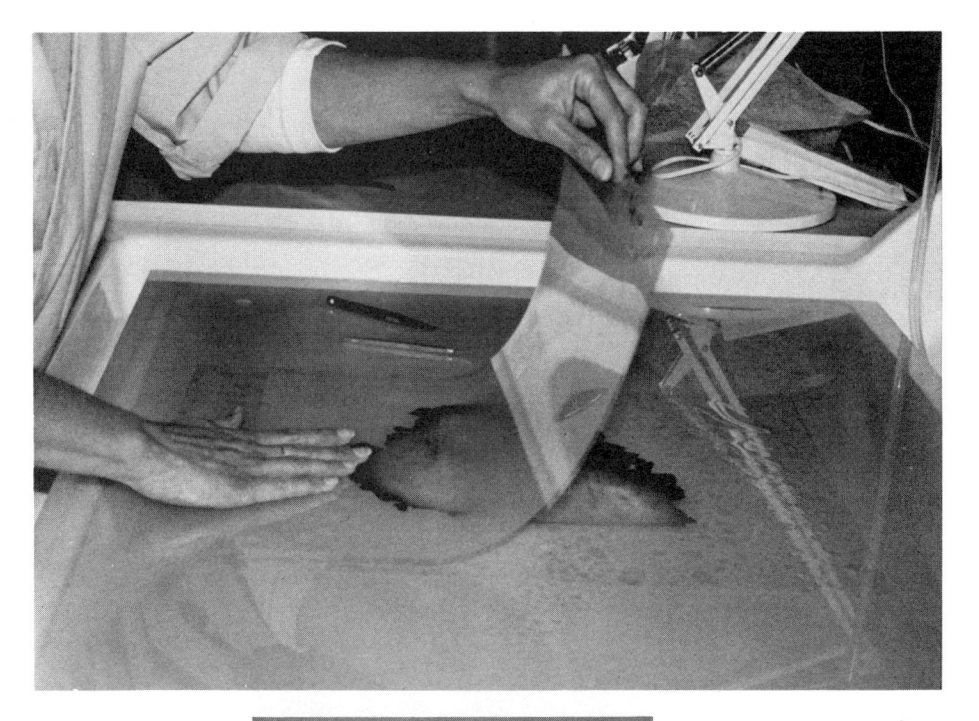

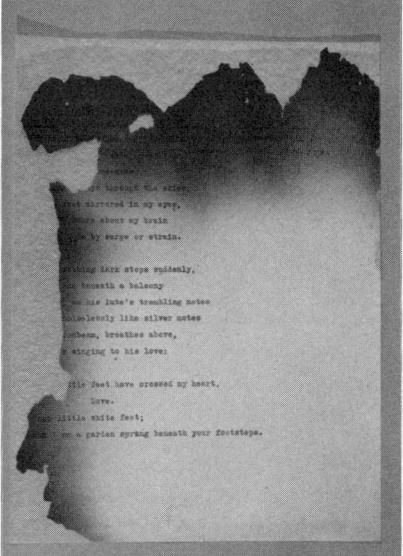

Fig. 8 (above): Lining tissue being applied to the back of a fragment on light table. Fig. 9 (below): After treatment, lined leaf from "The Marionettes" with smaller fragments reattached. See "before" treatment, fig. 4.

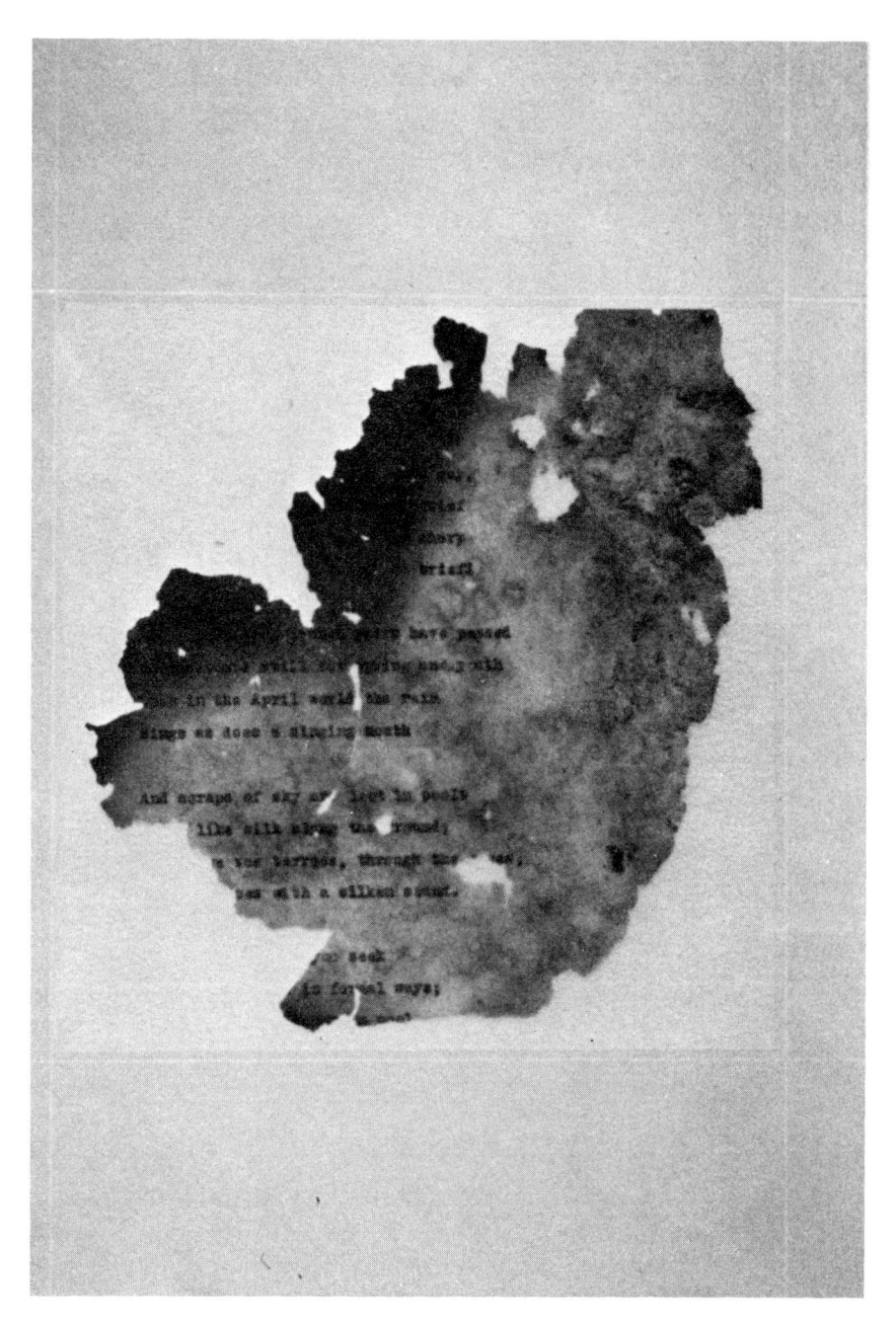

Fig. 10: Same fragment as in fig. 1 ("Eunice") after full treatment and encapsulated in polyester film. The finished product.

this condition the fragments can be presented to the scholar in a housing that allows for the viewing of both front and back of an item without visually obscuring any details of information. To date, approximately 75 of the 287 fragments have been treated completely or are in various stages of treatment. As might be expected, such care requires many hours of meticulous attention, with treatment averaging from 5 to 10 days per leaf. Since the treatment procedures are constantly being refined as new techniques are discovered and new information becomes available, it is hoped that the improvement in these procedures will aid in the timely completion of this ambitious and critical project.

Jill Whitten, during her conservation internship, is shown testing pigment areas with distilled water and solvents to find an appropriate means of cleaning an untitled painting by Al Held.

A Summer Internship in Paintings Conservation

By Jill Whitten

As a Conservation Technician at the Harry Ransom Humanities Research Center, my responsibilities include exhibition preparation and installation, housing of various collections, and minor treatments of paper artifacts. In addition to my duties as technician, I am also assigned as Conservation Liaison to the Iconography Collection, which contains the art associated with the HRHRC's literary holdings: prints, drawings, paintings, and objects. In my capacity as liaison, I am responsible for the maintenance of a wide variety of materials, even though my training in the Conservation Department has been primarily in the care of paper artifacts. Since the HRHRC does not have a paintings conservator on its staff, in the summer of 1988, to aid me in the maintenance of the Iconography paintings and to expand my understanding of the different conservation disciplines, I undertook an internship in the study of paintings conservation and survey methods, under the supervision of Sara McElroy, Head Conservator at the Archer M. Huntington Art Gallery at The University of Texas at Austin, who holds an M.A. from SUNY-Cooperstown with a specialty in Paintings Conservation.

Having been involved with the Conservation program for over two years, I am aware of some of the types of damage which may occur to paintings from being mishandled or stored in poor environmental conditions. Although I had no experience in comparing the problems found in modern paintings to those found in older, more traditional works, I was particularly interested in this type of investigation because the Iconography Collection contains both. Another reason for the internship was to learn methods of surveying the condition of paintings, since in the next few months I would participate in a condition survey of the Iconography paintings. The objective of such a survey is to provide an overview of the physical condition of the paintings within a collection and to identify immediate and potential problems.

The first five weeks of the internship were spent in the Huntington Art Gallery learning paintings survey methods and terminology. Thirty-eight paintings executed in the 1960s were surveyed in the Gallery's exhibit "Exploring the 60's—Selected American Paintings from the Michener Collection." A survey form describing the material of the support, ground and paint layers, surface coating, and the method of framing was filled out for each painting. In addition, each painting was measured and carefully inspected in normal and raking light (a beam of light cast horizontally over the surface of an object to illuminate planar irregularities). The condition of the support, ground and paint layers, and surface coating was then described in detail, and a recommendation on the care and possible treatment included in the written documentation.

The terms "support," "ground" and "paint layers," "surface coating," and "framing" refer to the different components of a painting. The "support" is the material to which the pigment has been applied. In the case of the paintings inspected at the Huntington, this material was cotton or linen canvas for the modern paintings, and wood, copper, or linen for the older paintings. The "ground" is the layer that is used to separate the support from the paint layer. Two types of ground are commonly found on older paintings: on wood-panel paintings, a combination of glue and chalk were mixed for the ground; for canvas paintings, oil and white lead (a pigment) were used as the ground. Modern artists often apply a ground layer of acrylic gesso, a commercial product that is pre-mixed. The "paint layer" consists of pigments mixed with an oil or a synthetic medium and referred to as oil paint or acrylics, the latter having been developed in the 1950s. Occasionally, the support and paint layers are not separated from each other by a ground layer, which is referred to as painting on "raw" canvas; canvas without a ground or pigment layer is referred to as "exposed" canvas. "Surface coating" refers to a coating that may appear on top of the paint layer. Many paintings, especially more traditional ones, are sealed with some type of surface coating, generally a natural resin varnish, although many synthetic resins are now in use. In addition to these components, each canvas painting was attached to an "auxiliary support": a wooden structure called a "strainer" or "stretcher." A strainer consists of boards nailed together to make a frame-like structure to which the canvas is nailed or stapled. A stretcher is also constructed of wood but is generally fitted with screws, wooden keys, or pegs, which allow the tension of the canvas to be adjusted. Paintings often become slack over time and for this reason in many cases a stretcher is preferred over a strainer.

The condition of the paintings surveyed varied a great deal. Many of the works traveled extensively in the 1970s, on loan to other institutions and galleries, and have suffered as a result. Some were in very good condition; others exhibited damage that included overall grime, stains, scratches in the paint, cracking, flaking, and loss. (A "loss" refers to missing areas of the pigment or the support.) Many of the works were painted with a very thick impasto, and the canvas had become severely quilted (puckered) on the reverse. Finally, some of the works were inadequately framed; i.e., the frame did not protect the edges of the canvas because it was not the appropriate size or was improperly attached.

The last six weeks of the internship focused on the documentation, testing, and treatment of two Latin American and four contemporary American paintings scheduled to go on loan. In the following discussion I am including only those parts of the treatment that I myself performed or assisted with, and I would stress that none of these treatments should be attempted without the supervision of a trained conservator. First, each painting was documented before treatment in both written and photographic form. Next, the different pigments on each painting had to be tested to see if they were stable enough to withstand the required methods of cleaning. Pigments were commonly tested first with a dry cotton swab rolled lightly over the surface to determine if any pigment was transferring onto the swab. If there was no transfer of pigment, a swab moistened with distilled water, saliva, benzine, or naphtha was then rolled lightly over the same pigment areas. (Saliva can be a very effective solvent because it is a mild enzymatic solution and can sometimes be used safely to remove grime that will not respond to distilled water.)

Some of the paintings required more involved treatments than others. *Santa Rosa de Lima según Vásquez*, by Fernando Botero, was photographed, tested with various solvents, and cleaned using distilled water and saliva. The treatment of Enrique Tabara's *Región de los Shiris* included photodocumentation, removal of a wooden strip-frame, and testing for the proper cleaning solution. A pale yellow horizontal band of paint along the bottom (which was part of the abstract image) was cleaned of dust and lint with saliva. Other areas tested sensitive to distilled water, benzine, and saliva, and could not be cleaned. Also, the painting was very friable, that is, fragile and powdery, and not all of the dust and grime could be removed. When the painting was unframed, masking tape, which had been painted black, was found on the tacking edges (the portion of the canvas that is folded back and around the stretcher or strainer edge). This brittle tape was gently removed mechanically, and black wooden strips were later attached to the tacking edges to recreate the aesthetics of the original black masking tape. I then toned in the losses in the pigment with le Franc-Bourgeois acrylic colors, which are reversible. In the last twenty years, some conservators have moved toward the use of "reversible" treatments, which simply means that in toning the losses materials are used which can be removed without strong solvents that might damage the original paint.

The treatment of Philip Guston's painting *Alchemist* included cleaning the surface of dust and grime by gentle vacuuming (using a conventional vacuum with a very small nozzle) of the recto and verso (front and back), followed by cleaning with naphtha. *The Conversion*, by Conrad Marca-Relli, was a bit more complicated to treat because this painting consisted of canvas collage elements that had been adhered on top of a painting by artist Stephen Pace, who at one time shared studio space with Marca-Relli. *The Conversion* was executed in oil, but in many areas the canvas was left exposed, that is, unpainted. No surface coating was visible. Many pieces of the collage elements were becoming detached, and there was evidence of previous repairs. On the verso, thick wax had been applied in several areas, apparently in an attempt to readhere the loosened pieces. The frame was removed and the front and back were gently vacuumed. In this case, the painting was removed from its strainer because the strainer was not adequate to maintain the necessary tension of the canvas. The painting was then placed face down on a large table so that some of the wax could be mechanically reduced using a sculptor's metal spatula. Finally, the painting was restretched on a new stretcher.

Two other American paintings were also treated during this period. An untitled painting by Al Held was tested for surface cleaning with distilled water, benzine, and naphtha, and found to be sensitive in some areas. Knowing that the painting could not be cleaned with distilled water or solvents, I then vacuumed, "dry cleaned," and dusted the painting with a soft brush. When a painting is sensitive to water and solvents, at times it can be cleaned by "dry cleaning," a technique that consists of removing grime with eraser crumbs or dust. Eraser dust, which can be purchased or made by the conservator by grating an eraser, is sprinkled on a very small section of the area to be cleaned and gently rubbed with a brush. The soiled eraser dust is then discarded, since any dust remaining on the canvas can ultimately damage the fibers. Also treated was a painting by Sterling Spadea entitled *Michener Formal*, which suffered from cleavage (detaching paint). Beva 371 (a synthetic resin adhesive) was applied to set down the insecure areas, and le Franc-Bourgeois acrylic colors were used to tone in the losses.

During these treatments, tiny fiber samples removed from several of the canvases were analyzed to identify the fiber type. Slides were made by separating these fibers, moistening them with distilled water, and placing them between thin glass plates. The slides were then inspected using a polarizing light microscope, and the fibers were observed to be of cotton, linen, or bast (hemp or jute). We then compared our samples with those on slides and in fiber reference books to make a conclusive identification. It is useful to identify the fiber type because some fibers react differently to humidity and others contain impurities, both of which can affect the paint layers on the canvas.

The final week of the internship was spent in the inspection of fifteenth- to seventeenth-century paintings on wood, copper, and linen. Examination under ultraviolet light often revealed evidence of previous restoration. The use of ultraviolet light will cause retouching, as well as various kinds of varnish coatings, to fluoresce differently and permit the distinction to be made between older and newer applications of these materials.

Because my training has been primarily in the care of paper artifacts, I noticed that some of the treatments performed on modern paintings, such as removal of stains from the support or dry cleaning, were actually more similar to those used in paper conservation than to those performed on traditional paintings. Although we did not have ample time to execute many of the treatments commonly performed on older paintings, I was able to do some reading recommended by Sara McElroy, and we discussed a number of the techniques described in the books. For example, a frequent problem with older paintings is discolored or dirty varnish that must be carefully removed with solvents and a new coating applied. Another common treatment on some older paintings is called a "strip-lining" and consists of adhering canvas strips to the tacking edges of a painting that have weakened due to abrasion. In this procedure, the painting must be unframed and laid on a clean, flat surface; a synthetic resin adhesive, such as Beva 371, is often used to apply the reinforcing strips.

This before-treatment raking-light photograph of the reverse of Conrad Marca-Relli's *The Conversion* illustrates how the painting is attached to a wooden strainer that does not provide adequate support for the painting. Linen-canvas strips were attached to the edges of the canvas to increase the tacking margins in order to allow for restretching.

Surveying the many different paintings in the Archer M. Huntington Art Gallery enabled me to compare the wide variety of problems that can occur in modern canvases to those more common to paintings produced before the twentieth century. In more modern paintings, the use of thick layers of paint that have not been allowed to dry, unprimed canvas, inadequate strainers, and non-traditional materials can contribute to deterioration of the artworks. While poor environmental conditions and an extremely active loan schedule can accelerate the deterioration of modern canvases, the damage found on the older paintings, such as abrasion and loss, is due more to aging and mishandling. The effects of unsympathetic treatment by previous restorers have also taken their toll. On the other hand, the very careful preparation and the techniques employed by the artists of the older paintings we inspected have resulted in their wearing fairly well over the centuries. The summer internship was an invaluable opportunity to learn about the care and

After-treatment raking-light photograph of the reverse of Conrad Marca-Relli's *The Conversion* showing the painting attached to a new stretcher that allows for adjustment of the tension of the canvas.

treatment of both modern and older paintings, and the techniques I acquired will serve me well in better assessing the results of the upcoming survey of the HRHRC's Iconography Collection paintings and in developing a sound plan of action for their future maintenance and preservation.

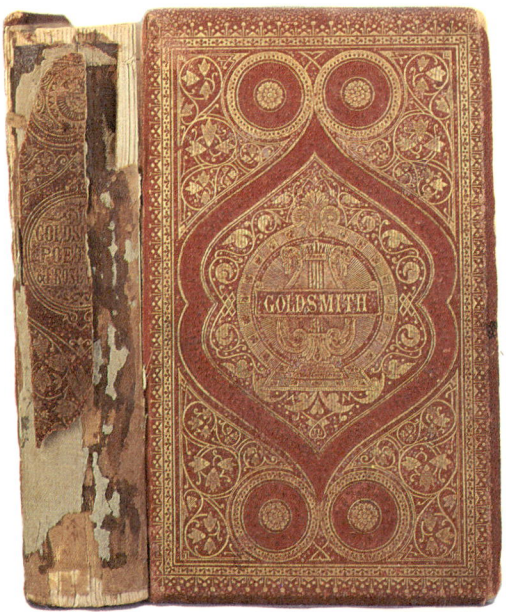

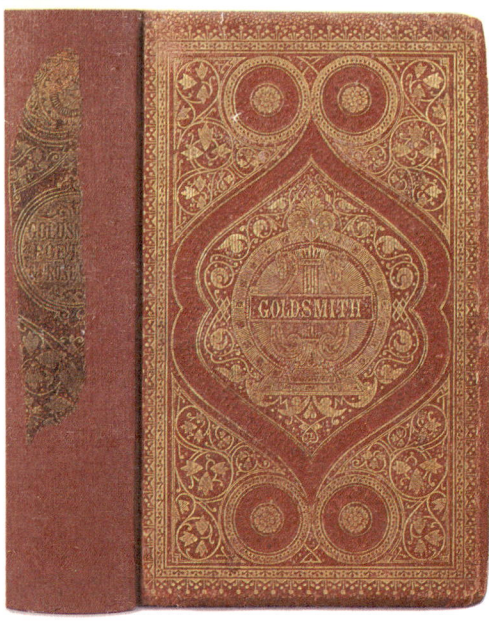

The Poetical and Prose Works of Oliver Goldsmith (ca. 1840) before and after conservation treatment. Above: note damage to spine and corners of the board. The initials "JL" are visible in an inverted heart under the lyre on the front board. Below: note the reinforcement of the case with new cloth, and the fragment of original spine cloth readhered to the new spine cloth.

Treatments for Five Nineteenth-Century Cloth Case-Bound Books

By Mary C. Baughman

Conservation treatment of a rare book may involve alteration of its artistic and structural integrity, and for this reason curators and conservators must consider a number of factors before a decision is taken to treat an artifact. The interests of scholars must also be included in the deliberations because historical or structural information that a volume provides in its unrepaired condition may be obscured through a conservation treatment designed to improve handleability or to retard deteriorative processes. In general, depending on the condition of the book, the treatments appropriate for the particular volume, and the needs of the scholarly community, a choice is made between intervention and non-intervention. For some damaged books, a protective housing is constructed and the book is left untreated, but any book in danger of rapid and drastic deterioration, such as that caused by insect infestation or exposure to moisture, will receive immediate conservation treatment.

Once the curator of a rare-book collection has determined that a volume is in need of treatment, the conservator examines the book and explains the options to the curator. In considering the amount of time needed to complete a complex treatment, the curator will weigh the benefit for an individual volume against responding to other conservation needs throughout the collection. Following the curator's decision on the level of complexity for a treatment, the conservator proceeds in such a way as to allow future conservators the possibility of reversing the treatment in the event that a better method is developed at a later date. However, some treatments, such as dry cleaning, which may seem relatively "simple," are inherently irreversible.

Nineteenth-century cloth-covered case-bound books in the collections at the Harry Ransom Humanities Research Center exhibit numerous features that call for special considerations in choosing an appropriate conservation treatment. Five books representative of the development of this edition binding structure during the period between 1820 and 1870 were selected for treatment in the Book Conservation Lab of the HRHRC: *Banks, Banking, and*

Paper Currencies (Boston, 1840), *The Poetical and Prose Works of Oliver Goldsmith* (London, ca. 1840), *London Labour and the London Poor* (London, 1861), *The Bridal Souvenir* (London, ca. 1850), and *The Amulet* (London, 1828).[1] The various treatment options available for each were reviewed and decisions made on the basis of the unique conditions and qualities of the individual volumes.

The deterioration of nineteenth-century cloth case bindings is partly a result of their structure, which was a departure from previous methods of bookbinding.[2] From approximately the tenth to the nineteenth century, most European books were bound by sewing their textblocks onto supports made of a vegetable fiber cord or of animal skin. Textblocks were first composed of papyrus or vellum, later of paper made from cotton and linen rags. The sewing support materials extended from both sides of the spine of the textblock and were firmly attached to boards, often by lacing the supports through the boards. Early boards were made of wood, and subsequently of laminated layers of paper. The spine and boards of the textblock were covered with paper, vellum, leather or tawed skin, seldom with cloth. Generally the covers were decorated after their attachment to the textblock. Each step in the production of a bound book required the hands-on skill of a craftsman, and each book was produced virtually one at a time.[3]

With the advent of the Industrial Revolution, the cloth-covered case binding was adopted in England and spread quickly throughout the Western world.[4] In this process, the textblock is sewn (at times without supports) and a lining material is attached to the spine of the textblock with an adhesive. Extending from the side edges of the spine, the lining material forms the main attachment of the textblock to the case, which is made separately by adhering

---

[1] R. Hildreth, *Banks, Banking, and Paper Currencies; In Three Parts* (Boston: Whipple & Damrell, 1840); *The Poetical and Prose Works of Oliver Goldsmith. With Life* (Edinburgh: Gall & Ingliss; London: Houlston & Wright, ca. 1840); Henry Mayhew, *London Labour and the London Poor: A Cyclopaedeia of the Condition and Earnings of Those That* Will Work, *Those That* Cannot Work, *and Those That* Will Not Work (London: Griffith, Bohn, & Company, 1861); *The Bridal Souvenir*, illuminated by Samuel Stanesby (London: Griffith & Farran, ca. 1850); and *The Amulet; or Christian Literary Remembrancer* (London: W. Baynes & Son, Wightman & Cramp, 1828).

[2] See Douglas Ball, *Victorian Publisher's Bindings* (Williamsburg, Virginia: The Book Press Ltd., 1985), pp. 1-9.

[3] See Gary Frost, "Codex Format Bookbinding Structures: A Survey of Historical Types," Supplement to *The Abbey Newsletter* (February, 1979): 39-42a, and Joseph W. Rogers, "The Rise of American Edition Binding," in *Bookbinding in America, Three Essays*, ed. H. Lehmann-Haupt (New York and London: R.R. Bowker Co., 1967), pp. 138-144.

[4] See Ball, pp. 17-22; Frost, pp. 42a-42d; Rogers, pp. 148-158, 179-185b; and Edith Diehl, *Bookbinding: Its Background and Technique* (New York: Rinehart & Co., Inc., 1946), pp. 71-77. Frost's article contends that the case binding structure was first developed in Germany not later than the eighteenth century.

THE PARTS OF A BOOK

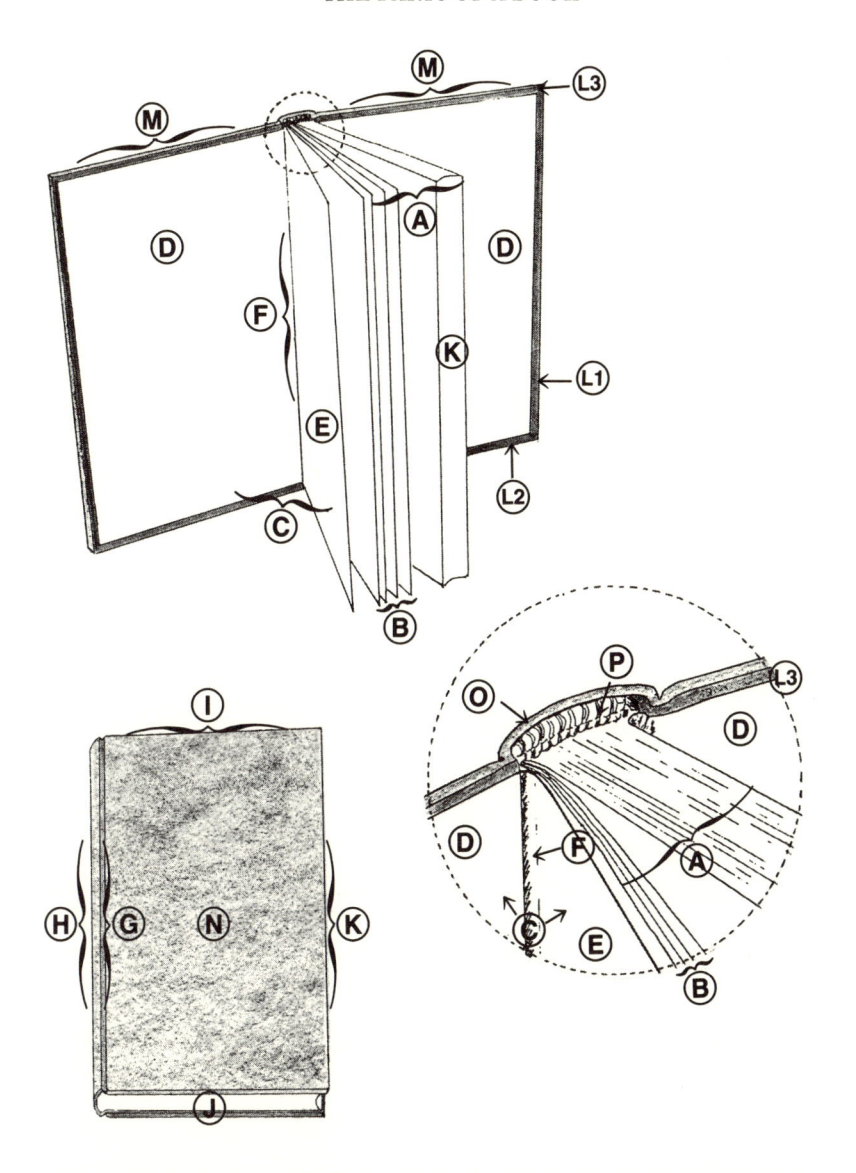

A: textblock; B: section, signature, or gathering (this is the first section); C: endpaper; D: pastedown (of the endpaper); E: free endpaper, or flyleaf; F: hinge; G: joint; H: spine of the book; I: head; J: tail; K: fore-edge; L1: fore-edge square; L2: tail square; L3: head square; M: boards; N: covering material; O: headcap; P: endband (headband in the illustration).

the boards to a covering material usually of cloth. The lining material and the endpapers of the textblock are then joined to the case, which is usually labeled and often decorated before it is attached to the textblock.

Today, most books are produced by a process referred to as adhesive or "perfect" binding (this publication is an example of the adhesive process). The spine folds of the sections are trimmed off after printing, and rather than

TWO TYPES OF SEWING STRUCTURE

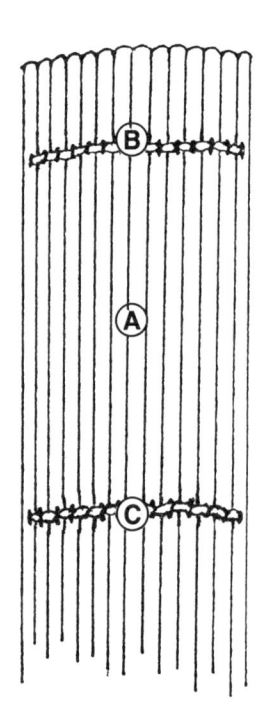

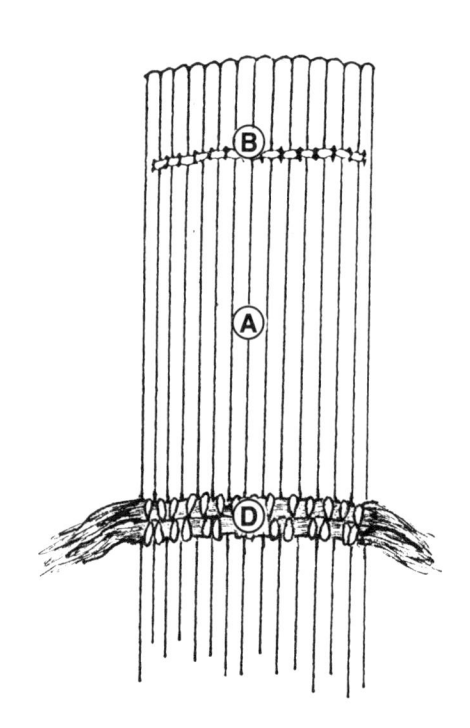

A: spine of the textblock; B: kettle stitch (unsupported); C: unsupported sewing for the textblock; D: supported sewing (the support is a pair of vegetable fiber [hemp] cords).

linking the sections by means of sewn supports, the spine edges of the textblock pages are joined with adhesive. After the pages are adhered, the textblock is then joined to a paper cover. Both the case binding and the adhesive binding are a product of nineteenth-century technology, by means of which thousands of identical books are machine-produced in a fraction of the time needed to bind one book by hand.

BOARD-TO-TEXTBLOCK ATTACHMENT

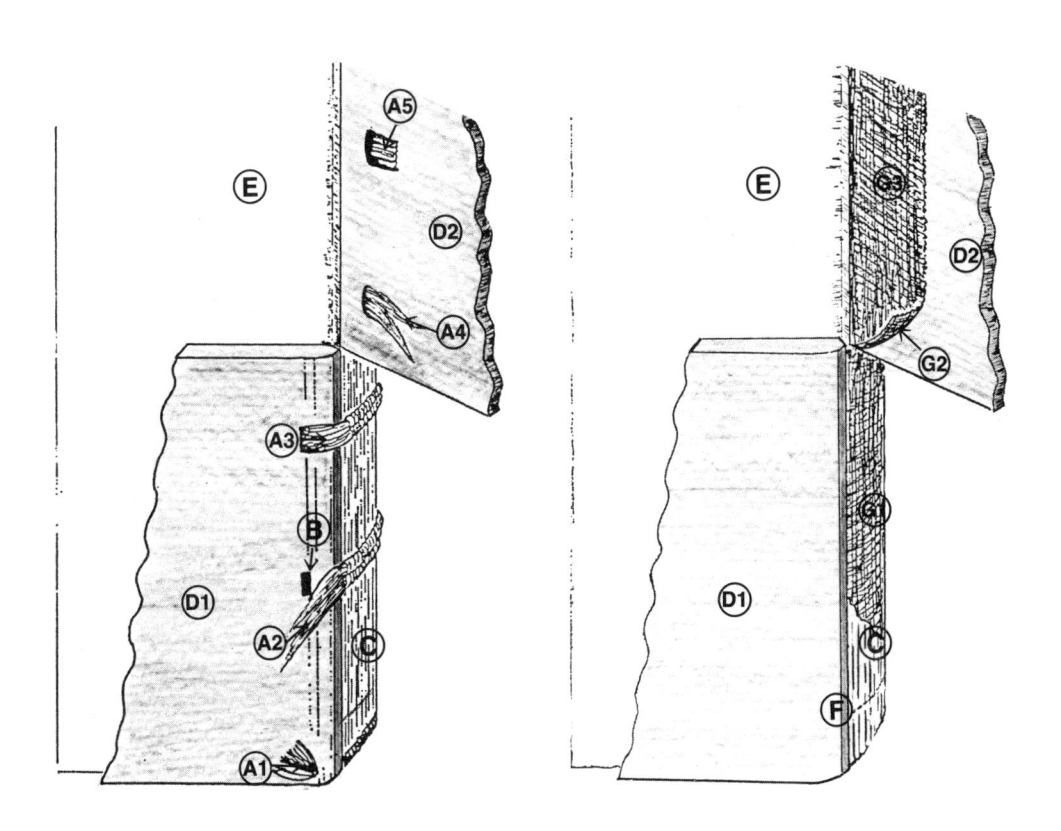

A1: sewing support (vegetable fiber cord), laced from the inside of the board to the outside of the board; A2: sewing support before lacing in; A3: sewing support laced from the outside; A4: sewing support laced from the outside to the inside, showing the inside before adhesion of the support; A5: sewing support, after lacing-in, adhered to the board; B: channel (for lacing-in); C: spine of the textblock; D1: board (outside); D2: board (inside); E: textblock; F: unsupported sewing; G1: spine lining material, adhered over the spine and tucked under the board; G2: spine lining material, before adhesion; G3: spine lining material, adhered to the inside of the board.

91

With the increased demand during the nineteenth century for cheap and mass-produced books, manufacturers experimented with new materials for making paper and adhesives.[5] Unfortunately, some of these new materials, such as the pulp used for manufacturing paper and boards and the components of adhesives, have proven to be chemically unstable.

In order to produce an inexpensive book that was both attractive and salable, the early industrial binders began to experiment with the use of cloth as the material for the case and with new techniques for decoration as well. Because untreated cloth is generally porous, it is unsuitable for covering books, but by 1828 experiments financed by Archibald Leighton were successful in producing a cloth with a "filling" or "size" which was impermeable to glue.[6] This type of cloth could be dyed evenly, and since the sizing stiffened it, decoration with embossing was also possible. A giant metal press, using tremendous pressure of up to 80 tons, heated positive and negative metal plate dies for embossing cloth or leather. Embossed by the roll, the cloth was then cut to size and adhered to the case boards; later, the cloth-covered boards were embossed to achieve a deeper impression and a more complex decorative design.[7]

The nineteenth century also saw the introduction of the profession of "book designer" when publishers and industrial binding firms hired artists to devise the designs engraved into the metal embossing plates.[8] Most book designers did not sign their work;[9] however, one of the most prolific designers, John Leighton (1822-1912), often made his initials part of a book's design. Three of the books examined in this article bear the initials "JL."

The combination of inferior structure, unstable materials, and decoration techniques which cannot be duplicated in a conservation lab generates a number of problems in the preservation of nineteenth-century cloth case bindings. In considering an approach for a book in need of treatment, the conservator first observes the condition of the volume, noting all existing weaknesses as well as each peculiarity that might require additional testing before a treatment could proceed. Any treatment that might change or destroy the historical or artistic integrity of a book must be weighed carefully before making a decision that could not be reversed by future conservators. In addition to such considerations as the effect of altering a binding structure that is damaging to the textblock, the advisability of removing stains, and the

---

[5]Dard Hunter, *Papermaking: The History and Technique of an Ancient Craft* (New York: Knopf, 1957), pp. 374-399, and John Carter, *Publisher's Cloth: An Outline History of Publisher's Binding in England 1820-1900* (New York: R.R. Bowker Co., 1935), pp. 14-17.

[6]See Carter, pp. 26-29, and Eleanore Jamieson, *English Embossed Bindings 1825-1850* (Cambridge: Cambridge University Press, 1972), p. 18.

[7]See Jamieson, pp. 27-29; Rogers, pp. 159-178; and "A Day at a Bookbinder's," Supplement to *The Penny Magazine* (September, 1842): 383.

[8]See Ball, pp. 66-67.

[9]See Ball, pp. 70-72, and Carter, pp. 46-48.

expedience of replacing support materials or of refurbishing the cloth coloring or replacing lost areas of cloth or paper, the artistic vision of the designer must also be kept in mind.

The first book treated in the Book Conservation Lab, *Banks, Banking, and Paper Currencies*, published in Boston in 1840, is a volume representative of the style of binding used in the developmental period of case binding in England during the 1820s. The fact that this book was bound in an earlier style—one that features a quarter cloth binding with paper sides—indicates how American binding practice at first lagged behind that of the English.[10] When this volume was received for treatment in the Conservation Department, it was observed that the paper covers were stained and worn from abrasion and the corners of the boards were crumbling. The cloth spine, made from an early embossed book cloth, was worn, faded, and had small losses at the head and tail. Also, the cloth was beginning to split in the joints at the head and tail; the paper label on the spine was abraded and missing parts; the endpapers were stained and dirty; and the front free endpaper had been torn out, causing damage to the next leaf at the head. The textblock paper, of a medium weight and fairly flexible, was foxed and stained along the hinge of the book.[11] Finally, the sewing of the third section was broken near the head edge.

Because the binding structure was sturdy, it was left intact. The loose section did pose a problem for future use of the book, but the sewing kerfs were large enough that it was possible to reinforce the sewing of the section without removing the spine cloth.[12] To mend the torn leaf and replace the missing free endpaper, a paper compatible with the remaining endpaper was selected and attached with paste.[13] To reinforce the joint areas and the head and tail of the spine, the cloth case was cut at the inside edge of the board and a small area of the cloth on the outside of the board was carefully lifted, after which Japanese paper tinted with watercolor and sized with an acrylic sizing was inserted under the cloth on the spine.[14] The original cloth was then laid back into place. Much care was taken in this operation so that the delicate embossing of the cloth would not be destroyed. To protect the book from further damage, it was enclosed in a polyester film jacket and this in turn was deposited in a specially built phase box.[15]

[10]By the 1850s, American manufacturers surpassed the English in the development of machines to speed the processes of edition binding. See Rogers, pp. 145-185b.

[11]"Foxing," a general term for stains, specks, spots, and blotches in paper, occurs in many forms. See Matt T. Roberts and Don Etherington, *Bookbinding and the Conservation of Books* (Washington, D.C.: Library of Congress, 1982), p. 109.

[12]Kerfs are sewing stations (or holes) which have been sawn into the backs of the textblock and through which the sewing thread passes.

[13]In most cases, precipitated wheat starch paste was the adhesive used for the treatments discussed in this article.

[14]Sizing is, in this case, the use of a waterproof solution to seal the pigment into the cloth or paper to prevent the pigment from bleeding should the cloth be exposed to moisture.

[15]For a discussion of the phase box, see pp. 149-155 of this publication.

Banks, Banking, and Paper Currencies (1840) before and after conservation treatment. Above: note the crumpled and torn cloth at head and tail of the spine, and the damaged corners. Below: note the reinforced spine cloth and the consolidated corners.

The second book, *The Poetical and Prose Works of Oliver Goldsmith*, is in a cloth case binding with a design probably created in the 1840s. The initials "JL" can be seen in an inverted heart at the bottom of the central motif on the front cover. This volume exhibited heavy embossing and bevelling of the boards, gilding on all edges of the textblock, and a gold design stamped on the front board and on the remaining fragments of the severely darkened and damaged spine cloth. Despite the nearly detached front board, the distorted shape of the spine, and the losses in the cloth, there was only one loose section near the center of the textblock, as well as a few detached leaves from the front and back of the book that still remained with the volume. On all edges of the boards, the corners were damaged and the cloth was frayed.

The volume's textblock, a lightweight paper of a pale tan color, was somewhat darkened on the edges. Throughout the text there were etched illustrations on a heavier weight paper of a paler tan color. A curious feature of the pages with etchings was the staining that appeared at the head and fore-edge corners of these pages but was not visible on the adjoining text pages. There is no evidence in the book to suggest that the etchings were removed from another copy and inserted into this book to form a "made up copy." These stains may have occurred before the book was bound, while the etchings were in a stack separate from the text. Perhaps the book was exposed to poor storage conditions, and high humidity or direct exposure to moisture affected the paper of the etchings more than that of the text. To a scholar these stains may have a bibliographic significance, of which the conservator is unaware.

Washing, the most effective treatment for stain removal, requires that the textblock be completely taken apart. After washing, the textblock is mended, then resewn. As well as removing stains, washing strengthens paper by rinsing out some of the products of degradation. But removal of the stains in the paper of *The Works of Oliver Goldsmith* would have destroyed evidence of the volume's provenance, and it also would have been necessary to destroy the sewing structure. Since the paper appeared to be of fairly good quality and strength, and the stains were not overly disfiguring to the illustrations and seemed to pose no threat of further damage, it was decided to leave the stains untreated.

In order to replace the spine cloth of the case and to reinforce the board-to-textblock attachment, both boards had to be detached from the textblock. Next, the fragment of original spine cloth and the remainder of the old spine lining were carefully lifted from the textblock. Because the sewing tapes and thread were not damaged by this procedure, reinforcement rather than replacement of the sewing structure was possible. New spine linings of Japanese paper and lightweight linen were adhered and the sewing of loose sections was reinforced through the linings. During the relining procedure, the distortion of the spine was corrected by reshaping it to its original curve. In place of the old tapes, the extension of the linen lining served to attach the textblock to the case. The loose pages at the front and back of the book were then mended and hinged to the textblock with Japanese paper.

The volume's endpapers, made of a paper similar to that used for the etchings, were soiled and damaged along the hinges. Two cloth-tape sewing supports had torn through the pastedown of the front board, detaching this board from the textblock. On the pastedown side, the endpapers were colored with a pale yellow pigment. Acrylic paint on a thin Japanese tissue proved to be a good match in color and weight for mends to the endpapers along the hinges.

Along the spine edges and at the corners of the boards, the old case cloth was lifted with care to avoid damage to the embossed boards and cloth. Paper pulp was then added to replace missing board and the delaminated board was consolidated with adhesive.[16] Watercolors with an acrylic size, applied to the same lightweight linen used to line the spine, provided the best match to the color and finish of the original cloth. This new cloth was laid underneath the original to reinforce the board edges and to serve as the new case cloth in the spine area. A lining of soft, flexible archival quality Western paper, adhered to the inside of the new linen, furnished support for the spine of the case. Once the book was cased in, the fragment of the original cloth was adhered to the new spine cloth in its former position. (See photos, p. 86.)

An element of the old structure was modified when the ends of the cloth tapes were cut off, when the fragments of the old spine lining were removed, and when the extension of the new linen spine lining was used to adhere the textblock to the case. These treatment procedures are not reversible. However, even though the missing spine area of the case cloth and the lining of the spine were replaced, and some original materials were reinforced with new materials, these treatment procedures could be reversed by future conservators. All other original materials of the book were left unchanged. While it is obvious that the book has been treated, the treatment does not detract from the artist's original conception. Structural changes in the book were intended to make it safely usable, and evidence of the book's original structure is preserved with documentation of the treatment.

When *London Labour and the London Poor*, another book with a cover design bearing the initials "JL," was received for treatment, the cloth covering of the case was frayed on all edges, very soiled, and unevenly faded in some areas but darkened in others. The spine cloth was darkened and torn in several areas, and the upper half of the back board showed a magenta color, while the rest of the cloth was of various shades of brown. Such uneven coloring is probably the result of poor storage, particularly excessive exposure to sunlight and dirt or soot. In some areas of the bevelled and embossed boards, the cloth

---

[16]Consolidation is the readhering of the delaminated layers of a board, and where necessary, infilling with paper pulp. For board consolidation, polyvinyl acetate emulsion glue (PVA) was mixed with paste and paper pulp to approximate the consistency of the original board.

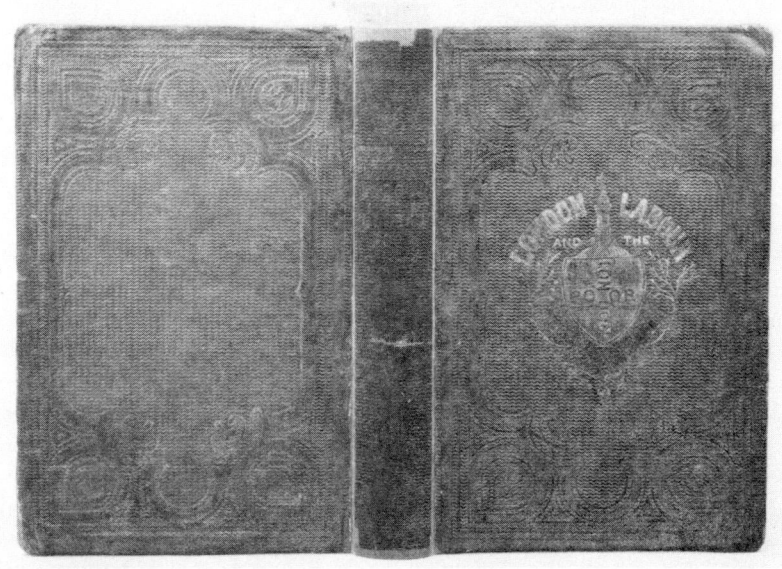

London Labour and the London Poor (1861) before and after conservation treatment. Above: note damage to the cloth at the spine and edges of the boards. The initials "JL" are visible in an oval at the bottom of the front cover design. Below: the cloth case has been cleaned, mended, and reinforced.

had puckered and lifted. Both the spine and the central design on the front cover, below which the designer's initials appear, still showed traces of gold stamping. The original color of the cloth case, a pale purple, was discovered by lifting the edge of the endpaper pastedown.

In treating this book, a test area on the spine was first dry cleaned with a soft brush. The same area was then cleaned with a methyl cellulose poultice, a chemically inert, viscous aqueous solution of cellulose which cleans the cloth without excessive dampness. Although most of the poultice was wiped off the cloth, the slight residue retained in the cloth appeared to replace the degraded sizing and strengthen the fabric. This treatment also eliminated a substantial amount of grime and appeared to be a safe method of cleaning the cloth, with the possible result of a more even color for the case overall. However, as the treatment progressed, it was discovered that the cleaning process was also removing some of the dye and gold stamping. More tests were conducted with various solutions of methyl cellulose and eventually the decision was made to clean the entire cover despite the likelihood of dye and gold loss. One reason for this decision was that, as noted above, the methyl cellulose treatment appeared to strengthen the cloth. Also, the cleaned cloth was a more even color, although it was still darker than the original pale purple, with the darkest and most evenly colored area appearing on the back board where the cloth showed the magenta shade.

The use of a bleach to lighten the darkened cloth was not considered because bleaches have been found to remain in the fabric, with the result that the chemical reaction continues and ultimately degrades the cloth. Instead, it was decided to apply color to the original cloth to give the case an overall shade matching the magenta area on the back board. Watercolor pigments are not reversible, nor was cleaning with a methyl cellulose solution. However, while the application of watercolor is merely cosmetic, the methyl cellulose treatment seems to have strengthened as well as cleaned the cloth. The outer appearance of the book has definitely been changed; and whether or not the change to the appearance of the book is an improvement is debatable. Because the techniques used are not reversible, the value of the treatment is also debatable. It could be argued that the artist's original conception has been altered by changing the cloth color. However, since the HRHRC has two complete three-volume sets of *London Labour and the London Poor*, which also show similar uneven coloring and damage to their cases, and since the single volume of this title treated in the Conservation Lab is the only remaining volume from an incomplete set, one benefit of this treatment is that the results can be used as a basis for future decisions in relation to the conserving of the other volumes.

The textblock of *London Labour and the London Poor* is composed of a thin paper that had become somewhat darkened along the edges of the sheets. No pages were torn or missing, though a few were loose at the front and back of the textblock, and the sewing was in good condition. The paper might have benefited from washing, but this procedure was not considered because of the desire to retain the original sewing, which would have been sacrificed in washing the paper. Using care not to disturb the original sewing, the old linings were removed from the spine of the textblock, and the spine was reshaped and lined with Japanese paper and linen. The old linings were removed because it would not have been possible to fit the book back into the case with extra linen on the spine. Also, extra layers on the spine would have made the book harder to open and would have placed stress on the paper when the book was read. The loose pages at the front and back of the textblock were then reinserted, and the sewing reinforced. Next, the textblock was reattached to the case with the extension of the spine lining. New linen was then tinted to match the tinted case cloth, and after consolidation of the corners, this new cloth also was used to mend the worn areas and to reinforce the spine of the case. Finally, the endpapers were mended and laid back into place.

The Bridal Souvenir is representative of the "gift book" genre of the 1850s and also bears the initials "JL." This book has a cloth-covered case with bevelled boards, an intricate embossed design stamped in gold on both boards and the spine, and a recessed border design on both boards made with either a turquoise pigment or a paper onlay. The endpapers are a stiff white paper bearing a design reminiscent of moiré silk, which is printed on the endpapers with a powdery white pigment. Instead of paper, the textblock is formed of single leaves of a medium-weight card, which was found to be so brittle that it tended to break rather than flex, especially in the hinge area. Each leaf of the textblock is elaborately printed in several colors.

As an example of a "caoutchouc" binding, the edges of the leaves of *The Bridal Souvenir*, instead of being sewn, were adhered to each other and then to a linen spine lining. The adhesive used contains rubber, which accounts for the name of this binding structure, since "caoutchouc" is the French word for rubber. Inherent chemical deterioration caused this red adhesive to crumble, staining the leaves along the spine edges and separating most of the leaves from the linen spine lining. The deterioration described is typical of this style of binding, which is a precursor to the modern so-called "perfect" or adhesive binding.

All of the leaves of the volume's textblock were removed from the cloth spine lining and dry cleaned along the spine edges using a soft powdered eraser to remove the larger accretions of dirt and degraded adhesive. Washing of the textblock was rejected because of the time it would have taken to perform the extensive testing required to ensure safe washing of the hundreds of colored inks used in printing the leaves. More importantly, in order for alkalizing agents to penetrate the thick card stock, a very thorough washing and buffering would have been required, and a prolonged washing might have

The Bridal Souvenir (ca. 1850) before and after treatment. Above: note damage to the cloth at the head and tail of the spine. The initials "JL" are visible just under the title on the front board. Below: the damaged cloth has been reinforced. The new structure of the book is not apparent from the outside of the binding.

damaged inks or caused delamination of the card. The leaves were next "guarded together," that is, joined in pairs to form sections, with a thin strip of Japanese tissue pasted at the spine edges of each pair of leaves. The newly created sections were then sewn through the folds created by the Japanese tissue, with four cloth tapes serving as sewing supports. After this, the new spine of the textblock was shaped and lined with linen. The tattered old spine lining, still showing traces of the powdery red caoutchouc adhesive, was removed from the case and filed with the documentation of the treatment.

To match the finish of the volume's original cloth, the worn areas of the case were mended with a lightweight linen tinted with acrylic paints. The endpapers with the powdery white moiré design were carefully lifted away from the case at the spine edge, and the linen extension of the spine lining was used to attach the textblock to the case. The endpapers were then laid back into place with very little loss of the friable surface.

This treatment involved a substantial change to the original structure of the volume. The attachment of the textblock was completely altered, but now the book opens easily without damage to the spine edges of the leaves, with the prospect that the new structure will prolong the life of the textblock. Except for the replaced spine lining, the treatment could be reversed if necessary, though it would be unwise to employ the older structure with the now embrittled leaves of the textblock. Unfortunately, an adhesive that would remain flexible through time and be easily reversible in solvents that would pose no threat to the delicate and complex printing inks does not, to my knowledge, presently exist. In any event, the old spine lining had to be replaced because it was already torn when the book was received and was completely split during the disbinding.

The Amulet is the first known example of the use of gold stamping on the spine of a cloth case binding. In *Victorian Publishers' Book-Bindings in Cloth and Leather*, Ruari McLean reproduces a photo of this book bound in purple silk; the HRHRC copy is bound in blue silk.[17] The color of the cloth on the HRHRC copy does not appear to have changed due to age or light damage; hence, this book is of interest because of the color of the silk, which demonstrates the variation in the cloth colors used for the binding of this "edition." In the developmental period of industrial binding, it was not unusual for manufacturers to make use of whatever cloth was on hand, regardless of color.[18]

The blue silk of the HRHRC copy is abraded on the edges of the spine and corners, and initially it was hoped that the old silk could be reinforced with new silk. Numerous experiments using modern silk were carried out to find an

---

[17]Ruari McLean, *Victorian Publishers' Book-Bindings in Cloth and Leather* (Berkeley and Los Angeles: University of California Press, 1973), p. 20. Although the image of *The Amulet* is reproduced in black and white, the caption states that the color of the silk is purple.

[18]See Carter, pp. 19-20.

adhesive that would hold firmly to a stress point, such as the joint, without marring the old silk during a moist or heat-activated application of the adhesive. Since the ideal of conservation treatment is reversibility, any adhesive used would also have to leave the cloth undamaged by its removal. Thus far no suitable adhesive has been found for adhering new silk to reinforce the worn areas on a silk binding, and thus it was decided to leave these areas frayed until such an adhesive could be found.

The front hinge of the volume was broken and the endpaper was torn in the hinge area. In the course of treating this condition it was thought prudent to reinforce the back hinge as well. The relative flexibility of the textblock paper and the soundness of the sewing precluded washing of the textblock. To reattach the textblock to the case, a lining was adhered to the spine and the case was adhered to the extensions of this lining. The front endpaper was then mended with a Japanese tissue. Because an acidic leather book plate on the front board had caused damage and discoloration to the first few leaves, this plate was removed and filed with the treatment report. A protective box was then constructed for the book and its use will be restricted to prevent further fraying of the silk.

It is instructive to compare and contrast the treatments considered and/or given to these books. Because the treatment of *Banks, Banking, and Paper Currencies* was minimal, were this book to be used frequently the treatment would not be sufficient to prevent further damage to the fragile spine cloth. However, in the controlled environment of the HRHRC Reading Room, supervision of patrons will ensure that this book is consulted with care. For the treatment of *The Poetical and Prose Works of Oliver Goldsmith*, much new material was added to reinforce the old, including a new spine lining as well as new cloth for the case and for the corners. The treatments of *London Labour and the London Poor* and *The Bridal Souvenir* involved substantial changes to the books. The outward appearance of one volume was altered by darkening the color of the cloth, while the inner structure of the other was changed by replacing the degraded adhesive attachment of the text leaves with a more flexible sewn attachment. In both instances, there were reasons for choosing to alter these books, but the results make the advisability of such a decision still a matter to be debated. For *The Amulet* a part of the treatment was delayed until suitable materials can be found or developed to reinforce the frayed silk of the case. In every instance, the original books have been irreversibly changed in some measure. However, all the books shown in the "before" photos are still recognizable in the "after" images because the extreme alternative of providing a completely new case was not chosen for any of the volumes. Finally, none of the books was washed or buffered, so that in each instance there has been no improvement over the lack of strength and quality in the nineteenth-century paper used in printing these books. Temperature and humidity-controlled storage will retard the deterioration of the paper, but not as effectively as washing and buffering. Promising techniques for use in non-acqueous deacidification—now in the experimental stage—do not require disbinding of a textblock. Should these or other techniques prove successful, conservators will have new options for the treatment of materials containing acidic paper. With advances in conservation treatment techniques, it will become more and more possible to achieve the ideal of treatment reversibility, which is among the conservator's foremost considerations.

The Amulet (1828) after treatment on the inside of the volume. Treatment of the case was delayed until a suitable adhesive can be found.

A book conservator must remain cognizant not only of the structural integrity of a volume but of the various kinds of information each book contains. As products of the Industrial Revolution, the nineteenth-century cloth-covered case bindings are of special interest to scholars both for the literary content of such books and for the ways in which the aesthetic development of case decoration mirrors the tastes of the times. In addition, the case binding reveals the development of the modern publishing industry and its experiments with new materials and technology for mass production. It is the conservator's responsibility to preserve as much of this valuable information as possible. While no treatment is ever perfect, the conservator strives to find the best solution both for the book and for the research scholar.

Lyle Wheeler, the art director of Selznick International Pictures, is shown here viewing one of the storyboards created for *Gone With The Wind. HRHRC Theatre Arts Collection.*

Conserving Art for Traveling Exhibition: Treatment of a Storyboard

BY SUE MURPHY

When collection materials from the Harry Ransom Humanities Research Center are to be loaned for traveling exhibition, a wide range of precautionary steps must be considered by the Center's Conservation Department for the protection of each item against possible damage. Given the vulnerability of collection items traveling on loan, it is imperative for the Center to maintain high standards of preparation for materials that will be in transit and on exhibition. Even such customary types of preparation as matting, hinging, and framing are often reevaluated for objects on loan, and it is occasionally necessary to require additional or special preparation and conservation treatment. Paper items, such as prints or drawings, are particularly vulnerable while on traveling exhibition and thus require extraordinary precautions. The HRHRC's Theatre Arts Collection contains thousands of drawings executed on commercially produced illustration boards consisting of a good-quality sheet of cotton paper mounted to a poor-quality wood-pulp board. Among such drawings are those known as storyboards, which present a succession of scenes to be filmed for a segment of a motion picture. In 1985, a storyboard from the movie *Gone With The Wind* (1939), part of the Center's David O. Selznick Archive, was requested by the Smithsonian Institution Traveling Exhibition Service. This loan request dictated special care for the safety of the artifact in transit to three exhibition locations, as well as during its exposure to light for a total of seven months while on exhibit.

BACKGROUND/HISTORY

In creating a storyboard, an artist is guided by the film director in translating the movie script into a series of renderings that represent the sequence of scenes to be filmed. Usually in narrative form, the artist's visual conception indicates camera distances and angles that will depict the action and evoke the proper mood. Some directors have had very elaborate storyboards constructed for the filming of their movies, feeling that it is essential to have most sequences worked out in advance of shooting. Prior to actual filming, the director, the art director, the cinematographer, and at times the producer will hold meetings to review the storyboards. Occasionally the boards are used on location during shootings. The final scenes, however, are chosen during editing, and often the finished film does not follow the storyboard in every respect.

With the arrival of the Selznick Archive at the HRHRC in 1982, the Center acquired 9 storyboards, 4 of which are from the movie *Gone With The Wind*. Also in the collection from *Gone With The Wind* are over 100 tiny sketches that are unattached but may at one time have been positioned on storyboards. Since most of these drawings are interpretations of the burning of and the escape from Atlanta, one would assume that in view of the complicated production and the great expense involved in filming the city on fire it was necessary to have this particular scene well-defined before shooting. At the time that Selznick's *Gone With The Wind* was produced, Lyle Wheeler was art director of Selznick International Pictures and William Cameron Menzies was production designer. Together, Wheeler and Cameron supervised a staff of 7 artists who provided 1,500 watercolor sketches for *Gone With The Wind*. From these sketches, which indicated every camera angle proposed for the movie, 200 sets were designed and 90 were erected.

TREATMENT PROPOSAL

In October 1985 a *Gone With The Wind* storyboard (fig. 1) was brought to the HRHRC's Paper Conservation Lab to be prepared for traveling exhibition. Although normal procedure would have called for treatment of this storyboard in due course, the request for loan made it necessary to carry out a thorough examination of the storyboard's condition and to prepare it both for regular handling and for transportation while on exhibit. The item consisted of an illustration board, measuring 20 x 30 inches, to which were attached 12 smaller pieces of illustration board bearing watercolor drawings, each approximately 4¾ × 5¾ inches.

As is generally the case with modern, commercially produced illustration boards, both the larger and smaller boards were fabricated from a sheet of good-quality cotton paper adhered by means of a water-soluble starch paste to laminates or layers of poor-quality ground wood pulp. In places, watercolor extended from the smaller mounted boards over the sides and onto the larger illustration board that served as backing. In addition, there were pencil sketches on the larger illustration board in spaces between the various scenes depicted on the smaller boards. On examination, it appeared that the larger illustration board was in a deteriorated and fairly brittle state. Were the larger board to be held by one corner, it might snap in two and rip through the top laminate of drawing paper bearing pencil and watercolor drawings. Another fear was that the item could easily break in transit. Since the larger illustration board already had begun to stain the top sheet of laminate, conservators felt that this backing of the smaller boards should be replaced. However, before reaching any decision, it was necessary to examine more closely the content and state of the storyboard materials.

After removing a small sample of the core of the illustration boards, the fibers of this sample were prepared using the standard procedure as suggested by the Technical Association of the Pulp and Paper Industry. A solution of alkali followed by one of acid cleansed the sample and eliminated such additives as sizing or coating, which could interfere with the observable properties of the fibers. The fibers were then transferred to microscope slides, stained with Graff's C-Stain, and viewed through the microscope. The Graff's stain is particularly useful for determining whether lignin, an acid-producing material, is present in the fibers. Using this process, the fibers are identified

Fig. 1: This photograph shows the recto of the *Gone With The Wind* storyboard before treatment. The after treatment photograph appears on p. 114.

on the basis of the morphological characteristics of the cellular matter, as well as by their color when stained. In this case, the test revealed that the core consisted of lignified wood pulp.

The critical condition of the storyboards was directly related to the poor-quality, lignified wood pulp from which they were made. Lignin is an acid-producing product found in all woody plants, and plant fibers must be cooked and bleached effectively or the lignin remains to cause the paper or board to self-destruct. Permanence and durability, therefore, are frequently a result of the processing and treatment of fibers before fabrication. Because deactivation of lignin is an expensive process that is only used for high-quality papers, it was not surprising to find that the backing or core of the storyboard contained ground wood pulp of a very high lignin content. It was apparent from the brittle, brown appearance of the board, as well as from its fiber makeup, that the storyboard was in danger of breaking even under conditions of normal handling. Since the board was to travel extensively, conservators and curators determined that the backing should be removed and the top layer of paper should be remounted on acid-free board.

Fig. 2: The fact that the edge of the board of one of the small watercolor drawings bears original medium was a consideration in the decision to retain the backings on the small boards.

A very important consideration in the treatment of a working drawing is the potential loss of historical evidence of the artist's process. In an attempt to save as much evidence of the working process as the condition of the item would allow, the conservators and curators decided that, in removing the top layer of paper and remounting it, there should be no removal of marks or lines that may have occurred during the creation of the storyboard. Even fingerprints and smudges in the margins would be retained, for these traces from the artist's work are often unique to the format of such preparatory drawings, and therefore it is important that they be preserved, if possible. Likewise, the roughness of the storyboard material and the appearance of the ragged dark edges of the boards are inherent to this type of format. Since in certain cases watercolors had dripped or been brushed along the edges of the smaller boards bearing the drawings and onto the face of the supporting illustration board (fig. 2), the problem was to retain these drippings without risking damage to the drawings. It was clear, then, that to remove the backing from the smaller drawings would result in a loss of the watercolors that had dripped or been brushed along their edges. That is, to follow the same procedure adopted for the large support board would eliminate from the smaller boards some of the evidence of the working process. Fortunately, however, the small size of the watercolor drawings made them less vulnerable to breakage. Thus, the decision was made to leave the original backings of the watercolor drawings as they were.

TREATMENT

Before removing the backing from the top layer of paper on the support board, it was first necessary to remove the smaller boards with watercolor drawings from the larger support board. With most of the smaller boards, the brittle rubber cement holding them to the support board gave way easily, but three of these smaller boards proved quite tenacious. In these cases, the top layers of the smaller boards were very carefully separated from the lower layers, leaving only the lower ones attached to the support board. This was done using a metal spatula to separate the layers, and leave only a thin bottom layer still attached to the face of the board, which could then be removed by softening the adhesive with heat applied by means of a hot air gun. Once softened, the adhesive underneath the smaller boards was loose enough for these layers to be lifted off with the spatula.

Removal of the layers of the smaller boards revealed a very thick degraded adhesive on the support board (fig. 3) and on the backs of the smaller boards (fig. 4). Also discovered on the backs of the smaller boards was a series of numbers in graphite pencil reading 9 through 20. As positioned on the support board, all the smaller boards with watercolors appeared in their numerical order, although one board (fig. 5) disclosed that its original number (11) had been marked through and the number 14 written beside it. Also, the front of the drawing now numbered 14 (fig. 6) had the word "Out" written across it and underlined, which suggested that it had been pulled up from another position or even another storyboard. One other smaller board with its drawing numbered 12 (fig. 7) had evidently been adhered, pulled up, and readhered, since the old abrasion from the original adhesive showed on top of it a second coat of cement that was also degraded. These changes likely occurred during construction of the storyboard, when the designers rearranged the sequence of drawings. Photographic documentation of the storyboard during treatment recorded this valuable information, which would not be available once the smaller boards were reattached to the support board.

Occasionally solvents were also used to soften the dark, brittle adhesive. But before applying solvents to the boards, a test was conducted to determine the solubility of, first, the adhesive, and second, the affected media. A drop of several solvents was placed on the area of the attachment and blotted with a small cotton swab. If the color from the adhesive transferred to the swab, it was a clear sign that the adhesive would dissolve in that solvent. It was discovered by this process that the adhesive would dissolve in ethyl alcohol, petroleum benzine, and acetone. The next step was to test the drawing media for sensitivity to these three solvents. The graphite pencil marks on the support board of the storyboard were tested by rolling a small dry cotton swab lightly over an inconspicuous area of the medium. When there was no transfer of medium to the swab, it was an indication that the graphite was not sensitive to the abrasion of dry cotton. Then, using cotton swabs that had been moistened separately with the three solvents, the same rolling motion was applied to the graphite. No trace of the medium rubbed off using the petroleum benzine, but unfortunately, in applying the ethyl alcohol and the acetone, the graphite transferred to the swab, indicating the medium was sensitive to both. In addition to observing these results under normal vision, the entire procedure was viewed under the stereomicroscope to allow for detection of even the slightest transfer of medium.

Use of the appropriate solvents reduced significantly the degraded adhesive on the backs of the boards bearing the watercolors and on the front of the support board (figs. 8 and 9). Most of the dark, crusty areas could be removed by swabbing with ethyl alcohol and acetone, while the areas where the adhesive was still sticky responded to petroleum benzine. With deteriorating rubber cement, there are often layers of adhesive degradation. At times it was necessary, therefore, to remove the old cement by alternating applications of the different solvents. Since the solvents that dissolved the adhesive could also damage the medium, treatment called for a careful local application of the ethyl alcohol and acetone in order to avoid the pencil marks, or at least to expose the graphite to as little solvent as possible.

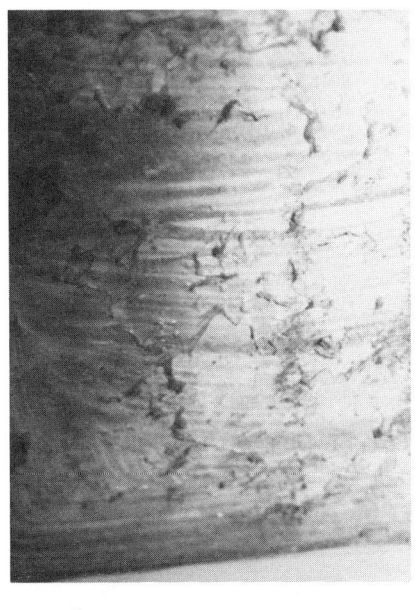

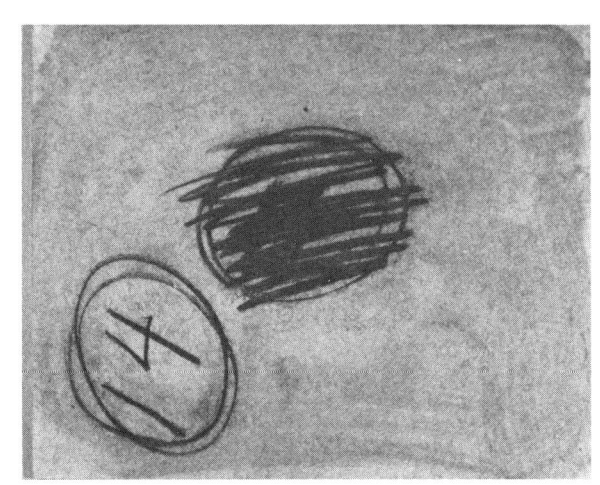

Fig. 3: In the upper left the front of the large support board is seen with a residual thick, crusty adhesive, which was revealed upon removal of the small boards. Fig. 4: The image in the lower left shows adhesive residue found on the back of the small watercolor numbered "11." Fig. 5: The image in the upper right shows how the numbering sequence was altered when a board numbered "11" was marked through and the number "14" written beside it. Fig. 6: At the lower right another change to the board renumbered "14" is seen on the face of the drawing where the word "Out" was written across the image.

After removing as much of the old adhesive as possible, the next step was to remove the brown, brittle core of the support board. The backing of the support board was first peeled down to a very thin layer. Then, once sufficient testing of the various media showed no potential problems with treatment using water, the backing that remained on the drawing paper could be removed by soaking the paper in a water bath. This procedure softened the starch adhesive holding the drawing paper to the core and allowed the poor-quality ground wood-pulp backing to float off into the bath. It was discovered

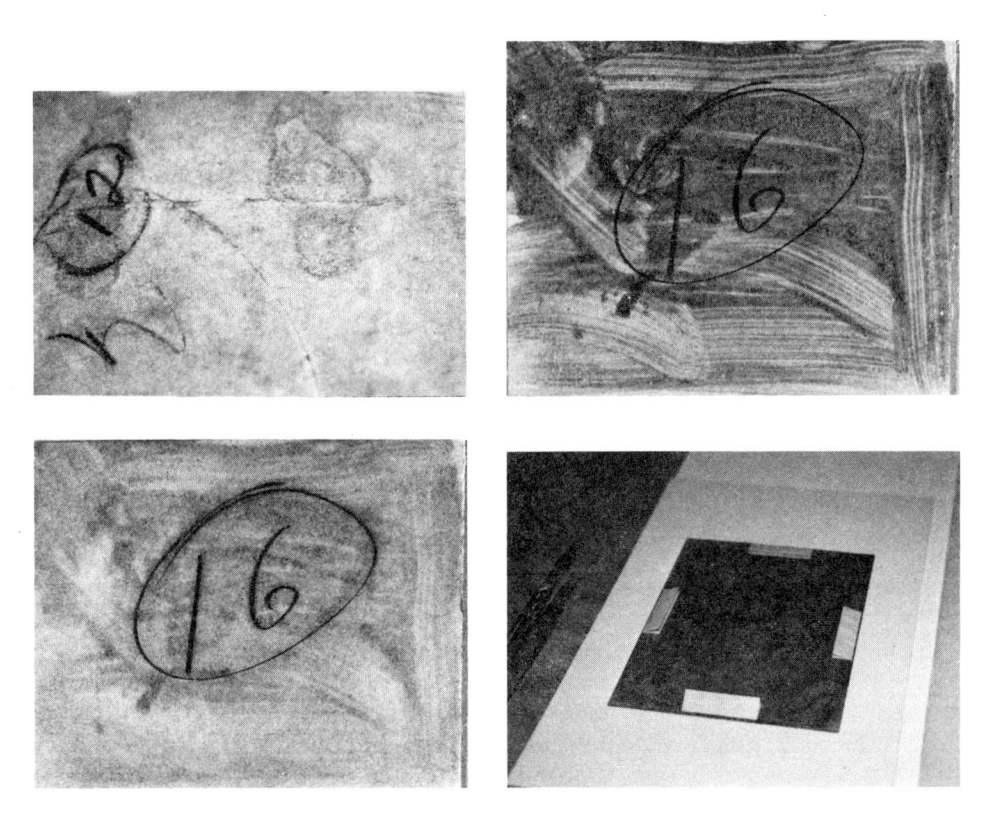

Fig. 7: The image in the upper left reveals further evidence of a change in the drawing sequence. The reverse of the drawing numbered "12" shows where it was removed from the support board and readhered, probably in another position in the sequence. Fig. 8: The verso of drawing number "16" is shown before the removal of degraded adhesive. Fig. 9: Drawing number "16" appears here after solvents were applied to reduce the residual adhesive. Fig. 10: This image shows hinges of Japanese paper as adhered to all edges of the watercolor drawing.

that the drawing paper that remained was stained and that the degraded adhesive had even created some transparent areas in the sheet. To reduce further a line of brown discoloration along the right edge, as well as stains from the adhesive, the paper was allowed to bleach in the sun. Through proper precautions sunlight can reduce some stains. To keep the sheet from drying out, it was placed in a tray on top of moistened layers of blotter paper and sprayed with an alkaline solution of magnesium bicarbonate. The paper was then exposed to the sun for approximately one hour. Afterwards, the sheet of drawing paper was taken back to the conservation lab where it was treated by soaking in several warm-water alkaline baths, which further reduced the discoloration.

The drawing paper then was ready to be remounted to a good-quality matboard. A very stable adhesive, as well as one of the simplest to remove, is starch paste. However, had the drawing paper been attached directly to the matboard using this water-soluble adhesive, the board probably would have bowed excessively from the moisture. Even if the board were successfully

Fig. 11: After the drawings were adhered to the large support board, weights were applied to the small boards to prevent warping during drying of the pasted hinges.

flattened, the layer of a very hygroscopic adhesive-like starch paste would cause the board to flex and bow unevenly during exposure to even slight changes in relative humidity. Therefore, the sheet of drawing paper was backed with a piece of lightweight Japanese paper attached with wheat starch paste and dried. Using a dry-mount press at a low temperature, the backed sheet then was attached to a piece of rag matboard with a very stable non-aqueous co-polymer heat-activated adhesive called Beva film 371. Were it ever necessary to remove the matboard, it would be difficult to separate the Beva™ film completely from the drawing paper without the use of strong solvents, most of which would dissolve the graphite pencil medium. For this reason, the Japanese paper backing would serve as a barrier between the drawing paper and the Beva™ film and allow for easy removal by water.

Next, the backs of the drawings were treated with an alkaline spray to help stabilize their acidic condition. Before readhering the drawings to the support

Fig. 12: This photograph shows the *Gone With The Wind* storyboard upon completion of the treatment.

board, the severed layers of the backing were reattached with wheat starch paste. The drawings then were adhered to the backboard using Japanese paper hinges attached with wheat starch paste, which would allow for easy removal at a later date, if necessary (fig. 10). After the drawings were adhered to the large support board, weights were applied to the small boards to prevent warping during drying of the pasted hinges (fig. 11). The final condition of the storyboard as it left the lab can be seen in the after-treatment photograph (fig. 12). Finally, the storyboard was placed in a sink mat, framed, and crated for shipping.

CONCLUSION

The Theatre Arts Collection at the HRHRC houses thousands of items rendered on illustration boards in a wide variety of drawing media. Not all the boards are in a condition as perilous as that of the *Gone With The Wind* storyboard. As members of the Conservation Department have inspected the collection, they have found that many of the drawing boards, though of poor quality, are tougher and less brittle than this particular storyboard. When possible, illustration boards are kept intact for the benefit of the researcher and also because remounting them is so time-consuming, especially for a conservation staff that has many items requiring urgent attention. Nonetheless, if the boards are extremely brittle, important to the collection, or frequently used, remounting is essential for the safety of the drawings.

At present the Conservation Department is compiling an inventory of various brands of illustration boards that form part of the Center's collections. This inventory will designate the collection, record the names of designers/artists, and provide a description of each item's condition, as well as photographing the reverse of the boards with the logos of their manufacturers. This information will assist curators of the Center's collections in making recommendations for conservation treatment and housing that will safeguard HRHRC archives against inherent self-destruction and the hazards of normal handling by researchers, now and for generations to come.

The first page of the HRHRC's copy of Jean Froissart's "Chronicles," Book I (circa 1379-1381). This illuminated manuscript on vellum is shown rebound using the "K-118" binding structure.

The "K-118" Binding Structure: A 500-Year-Old Experiment for Modern-Day Book Conservation

BY BRUCE LEVY

One major focus of the Harry Ransom Humanities Research Center is the preservation not only of the textual content of its collections but also of their bindings when they have historical or artifactual significance. It is the job of the HRHRC's Book Conservation Lab, in concert with curators and scholars, to provide patrons with "usable" collection materials, both rare and non-rare, and to protect such items by seeing to it that their texts and bindings are in stable and durable condition. At the same time, the Center's conservators are concerned that these materials retain as much of their original intent and ambience as possible. In seeking to make materials available while still safeguarding and preserving them for future use, book conservators at the HRHRC apply various treatments, which are undertaken with sensitivity to each item's unique qualities.

Collection materials at the Center span the entire history of the written word. Thus the book conservator is exposed to a wide variety of methods for holding together manuscripts or printed materials, from rolled papyri, through the simple and elegant coptic bindings with bare boards and exposed sewing, to the binding structures of today. The experience of treating so varied a collection affords the alert conservator opportunities to observe which structural elements in bookbindings were successful, and which were not; which materials have lasted for centuries, and which broke down over a relatively short period of time. By observing the intrinsic strengths and weaknesses of various binding structures, a conservator may be able to synthesize these elements into a hybrid binding that may solve specific modern-day book conservation problems.

For the sake of simplicity, bookbinding structures can be divided into three major categories: the "Rounded and Backed," the "Limp," and the "Hard-Board Conservation Binding." Within these categories, one may find anomalies of bookbinding structure, and it is among such anomalies that the conservator can discover new structural elements—new to us, that is. Equally important, the conservator can discern the ways in which an individual binder apprehended the relationship between textblock and binding.

The "Rounded and Backed" structure is the binding that library patrons encounter most often. After the sewn textblock is made round at the spine (and thus also along the fore-edge), it is placed in a press and shaped further with a hammer to produce the "shoulder" of the textblock. The cover boards are either nestled against the shoulder, or set slightly away from it, to form the familiar "groove" that acts as a hinge for the opening of the boards. (See diagrams 1 and 2.) The massive use of this structure by the printing industry is proof enough of its efficacy. However, the publishing industry's considerations rarely view the "life" or "importance" of a book as extending beyond the publisher-to-buyer transaction, though there are fortunate exceptions. With well-made paper and proper binding technique, the rounded and backed book will in fact allow for ample use before it requires the attention of the conservator, if and when the value of the book warrants attention as opposed to replacement. Nevertheless, the "Rounded and Backed" binding, while generally serviceable, has its weaknesses in relation to function and durability. When this type of structure is opened, the textblock receives most of its stress at the first and last few sections or signatures, for it is here that most of the flexion of the text paper takes place. (See photo 1.) With the embrittlement of the paper, due to poor production methods or environmental factors, one can expect a breakdown of the text at these stress points.

Another weakness of this structure, which many library patrons have observed for themselves, is the detachment of one or both of the cover boards from the rest of the book. The reason for this structural failure is twofold. First, the leather, paper, or cloth used as a cover material breaks down because of poor manufacturing methods and/or environmental conditions that accelerate the deterioration of the covering material. Second, the superstructure of the binding, which lies underneath the cover material, is not designed for the continual handling that it undergoes through library usage. Of course, one must not forget that many "bookbinding treasures" are created using this same "rounded and backed" structure, and there are "fine bindings" made with this method that have lasted for many years, whether handled often or just displayed, though many more that patrons are not permitted to examine because of their presently deteriorated condition.

The "Limp" binding structure is primarily a historic one, with its known use spanning the period from at least the fourteenth century up to the present. This binding category includes books with flat-backed textblocks and thin covers made of vellum or sometimes paper, without the addition of boards as stiffeners. (See diagram 3.) The result is a book that is lightweight and flexible even when closed. Also, with no rounding and no shoulder, the book can open without the flexion and stress of the rounded and backed structure. Originally developed for account books of the late Middle Ages and occasionally adopted by fine presses like the Doves Press Bindery, this method is rarely utilized today. Examples of the limp binding vary from plain vellum with no title to

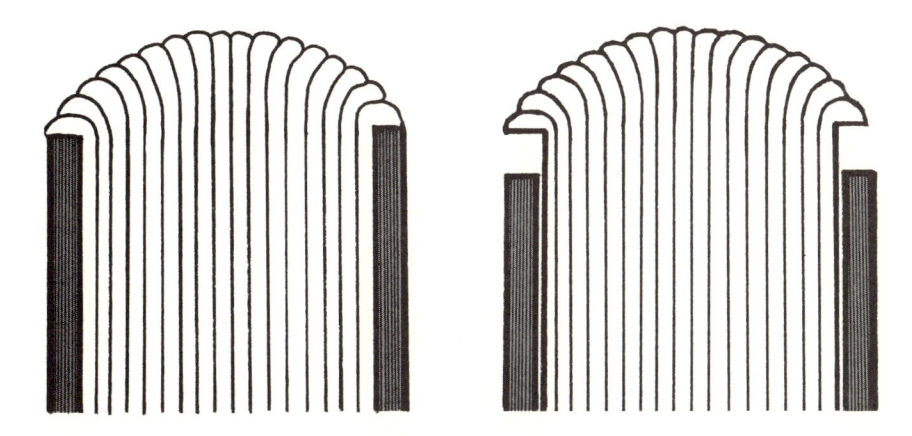

Diagrams 1 and 2: "Rounded and Backed" binding, illustrating cover boards nestled against or set slightly away from the shoulder. Photo 1: "Rounded and Backed" binding, showing a first signature where stress can cause breakdown of the textblock.

Diagram 3: "Limp" binding, illustrating a flat-backed textblock without boards. Photos 2 and 3: "Limp" binding, showing vellum textblocks of volumes in an upright, standing position or opened lying flat on the spine.

account books with elaborate lacings of leather thongs, the latter being objects of great beauty. Interestingly enough, the textblock surrounded by this structure has fared well during such disasters as the Florence Flood of 1966. While leather bindings became waterlogged and suffered from staining and mechanical damage, the limp books seem to have floated along unharmed. Although many of the limp covers were themselves destroyed in the flood, they yet provided adequate protection for the texts they covered.

Aesthetically, the limp structure makes for an elegant book that is pleasing to hold and use, with the patina that vellum takes on adding a special joy for the bookman. However, this binding does have certain inherent weaknesses. For example, large account books bound with a limp structure have not held up well, since their weight is too great for a binding that was not structurally designed to support its textblock in an upright, standing position. Originally, perhaps, these account books were stored on their sides, so that the weight of the text did not shift or press downward, as it does today when they rest on their edges on library shelves. (See photo 2.) Also, when constructed of vellum, this "limp" binding does not readily lie flat on its own when opened but tends to spring closed because of the stiffness of the vellum and of the structure itself. (See photo 3.) For this reason, the smaller limp vellum bindings have to be held open by the reader's hands, with the result that, in some cases, the resistance of this structure to staying open has caused its sometimes brittle sewing to break down. Another problem is the extreme reactivity of vellum to changes in humidity. When this type of binding is exposed to variations in humidity the consequences are, at the least, some cockling of the vellum and, at the worst, extreme convolutions of the cover material. Water can also cause the same damage, with the further risk of the vellum becoming horny and inflexible. Having performed its role in binding history, the limp structure can still serve on occasion as a valuable project for the modern book conservator, since it can expand his or her understanding of book function and form. However, other than as a facsimile binding, I do not personally see this structure as an answer to today's book conservation problems, unless, of course, one is expecting a flood.

The third category of current structures, the "Hard-Board Conservation Binding," can be seen as both an historic structure and a modern hybrid. This structure involves the use of heavy boards for the cover and thick thread for the sewing of the textblock. Examples in this category include the wooden board bindings in the "Nuremberg" style, typified by the work of binders who received commissions during the fifteenth and sixteenth centuries from German publisher Anton Koberger. Details of the "Nuremberg" style that distinguish it from other "hard-board" bindings are the inner bevel of the board edge, which accommodates the spine swell caused by the heavy sewing thread, and the outer bevel on the same edge both as a functional element, since there is no real shoulder to support a thick board edge, and as an aesthetic consideration. (See diagram 4.) This hard-board structure is excellent for large, heavy books requiring ample support from the binding. It can, however, still cause stress at the same points as the "rounded and backed" structure, but to a lesser extent because of a "minimal" shoulder. (See photo 4.) Also, though many binders are now intrigued by the beauty of polished wood boards found in one of the modern versions of this binding style, the dimensional and chemical instability of today's quickly dried wood recommends that the conservation binder should substitute laminated "conservation board" for the wood board cover. This substitution of "conservation board" will retain the feeling of mass given by wood boards while also providing the dimensional stability of lamination and the chemical nonreactivity of acid-free materials.

Among the HRHRC's "Nuremberg" bindings from the fifteenth and sixteenth centuries is the two-volume work entitled *Speculum Naturale*, which was bound in Nuremberg through Anton Koberger in approximately 1493, as evidenced by a printer's proof from Koberger's shop found glued facedown to a cover board on one of the two volumes. Printed in Strassbourg in 1481 by the anonymous printer of *Legenda Aurea* (also printed circa 1481), *Speculum Naturale* was written by Vincent of Beauvais, a French Dominican scholar who died sometime before 1264. In 1985 the HRHRC's copy of this two-volume work came to the Book Conservation Lab for restoration, and in researching its origins, John P. Chalmers, librarian of the Center's collections, discovered that Dr. Ernst Kyriss, in his book on German Gothic bindings, had identified the bindery by the finishing tools used for the design on the book's leather cover.[1] Dr. Kyriss designated the bindery "K-118," and thus the name now applied to this unique hard-board structure surrounding the HRHRC's copy of *Speculum Naturale*. (See photos 5 and 6.)

In consultation with the curator of the HRHRC's book collections, the first determination to be made was whether to preserve the present bindings, to replace their coverings with new conservation bindings, or to restore the book's original bindings. Inspection revealed that, because the bindings of this two-volume work were deteriorating, simply to preserve the coverings by housing them in protective boxes would not be a viable option. It was also agreed by both curator and conservators that since the bindings were of equal importance with the text, to replace the originals with conservation bindings would clearly reduce the integrity of the artifact. Furthermore, because the bindings on the *Speculum Naturale* volumes appeared to be an example of the fifteenth-century binder's craft, this too was a sound reason for restoring rather than replacing them. Choosing restoration was an unusual decision, for this procedure entails more care for, and understanding of, the item in question than does either passive preservation or conservation rebinding.

---

[1]Ernst Kyriss, *Verzierte Gotische Einbande Im Alten Deutschen Sprachgebiet* (Stuttgart: Max Hettler Verlag, 1954), II, 23.

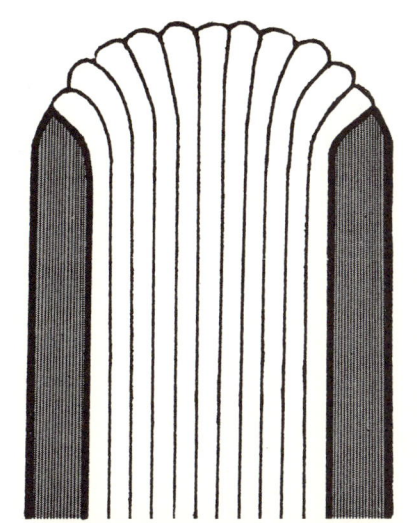

Diagram 4 (upper left): "Nuremberg" style of hard-board binding. Photo 4 (upper right): "Minimal" shoulder of the hard-board binding. Photos 5 and 6: Volumes I and II of *Speculum Naturale* before treatment.

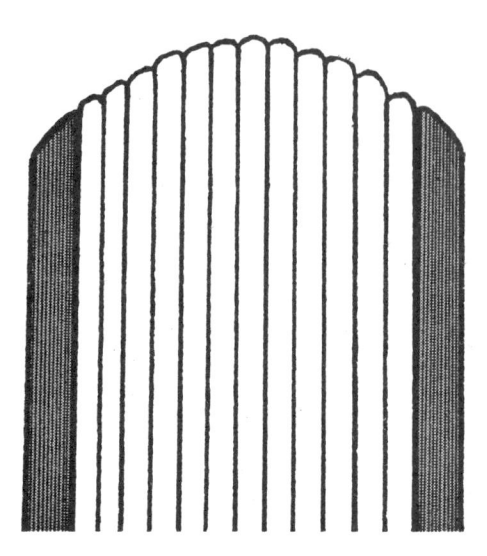

Diagram 5: "Nuremberg" hard-board binding, illustrating the continuity to the round of the spine. Photo 7: "K-118" binding structure, showing the two-sided attachment of flaps that create a clamp effect.

Thus, it was through this extraordinary undertaking that I first became aware of the "K-118" binding structure and the potential for its application to the practice of contemporary book conservation.

After the decision had been made to restore the bindings, I then entered the stage of documentation. This process involves a description of the item, a treatment proposal, and a final treatment report. Documentation is particularly important to a collection like the HRHRC's, for as conservators we are merely temporary caretakers of history. Just as there were caretakers before us, there will be others to come after us, and it is our duty to enable them to work from a position of knowledge of past conservation decisions. The need for documentation becomes more obvious in working on a piece that has been previously restored, especially when there is no documentation to which we can refer. In the case of the *Speculum Naturale* volumes, every stage of the restoration process was photographed to document the item before, during, and after the treatment. This method of documentation allows us to view each step of the process in relation to all the others and, in this way, to work more efficiently. Documentation also teaches us to see, which may be one of the more important aspects of book conservation.

The most striking observation was that the bindings for this two-volume work exhibited certain structural details which differ from usual elements found in the "Nuremberg" hard-board binding and which are, to my knowledge, entirely unique. For one thing, the board-to-text relationship was similar to the hard-board structure, with its minimal shoulder, but, in this case, the inside of the cover board was absolutely flat, and the text had no visible swell. A second observation disclosed how a shaping of the outside board edge gave continuity to the round of the spine. (See diagram 5.) This combination of structural elements allowed the pages to open from the first to the last without the flexion exhibited by the "rounded and backed" structure and the "hard-board conservation" binding. The final unique detail was an unusual method of lining the spine of the textblock with vellum before attaching the cover material. Ordinary procedure for either the historic or the modern hybrid model of the "hard-board" structure is to line the spine of the textblock with strips of vellum or linen between each of the sewing supports or cords. These flaps are then extended from the spine, to be attached later to the inside of the board. While this procedure lends strength to the text-to-binding attachment, the "K-118" structure improved on it by cutting each flap in two places, resulting in three tabs. By attaching the two outer tabs of the piece of vellum over the cover board and tucking the center tab under and onto the inside of the cover board, the "K-118" structure achieved a binding that will hold the cover in place even with the deterioration of its leather. In other words, by forming a two-sided attachment of the vellum or linen flaps, the "K-118" created a clamp effect that maintained the binding's structural integrity. (See photo 7.)

Further inspection of the books revealed that the binding had been restored previously because of the breakdown of the original sheepskin covering, primarily at the joints and edges, as would be expected. While the two volumes had been rebound in sheepskin, the later skin had deteriorated rapidly and even more dramatically than the original covering.[2] The leather used by the previous restorer was suffering from what in book conservation is called "red rot." Although the restorer retained most of the original sheepskin and onlayed it onto the newer sheepskin covering, he did not follow the same procedure with the original vellum spine lining. After removing the flaps attached to the boards, the restorer did not replace them, which contributed to the binding's rapid deterioration. This also meant that the three-tab vellum flaps had been discarded. Fortunately, however, there were still obvious indications of the "split-tab" placement of the vellum.[3] (See photo 8.) In restoring the original structure of the two volumes, I reintroduced the "K-118" split-tab procedure, and after the spines were lined in this manner I covered them with calf leather, inlaying the surviving pieces of original sheepskin cover into the new calf leather. I then fabricated new fore-edge clasps to replace the original pieces that were missing. At last the books were available to patrons without restriction. Of equal importance, these two volumes demonstrated in their finished state a flexibility and functional quality that is superior to many of today's conservation-style bindings. (See photos 9, 10, and 11.)

Recognizing the implications of the "K-118," I began the creation of a series of binding models utilizing this structure's elements to solve some common modern-day book conservation problems. In the process of binding such models, which are generally constructed for the benefit of the binder, one is able both to test functional aspects of a structure and to enlarge one's understanding of binding mechanics. The first model was a facsimile of the *Speculum Naturale* bindings, with the difference that for the cover I used alum-tawed pigskin, which is one of the most durable of covering materials. While alum-tawed pig is not a "leather" in the proper sense of the word, it is an attractive and remarkably strong material that is often used in conservation bindings for early books, and has repeatedly proven its durability.

Concurrently with this work, I developed a new style of fore-edge clasp. Original clasps are often missing from early bindings because of the loss of the nail-like rivets that hold them to the board. The new clasps I constructed are

[2]The difference between sheepskin from 500 years ago and modern sheepskin is so great that the latter can crumble away within 10 to 50 years while the older skin may remain in a usable condition for centuries.

[3]Apparently the restorer did not understand the superstructure of the "K-118" binding, probably never having seen such an anomaly before, and thus left out the split tabs entirely. Since this structure was new to me as well, I decided to build a model in order to study the binding as a way of replicating its unusual features. Only then did I become aware of the revolutionary assumptions made by the structure's anonymous binder.

Photo 8 (at top): "Split-tab" placement of the "K-118" structure remained evident from marks on the spine. Photos 9, 10, and 11: Volumes of *Speculum Naturale* restored in their original "K-118" binding structure, with new fore-edge clasps.

Photo 12 (at top): *Eusebius Chronicon* (1483) bound without clasps in the "K-118" binding structure. Photo 13 (in middle): *Sermones de Laudibus Sanctorum* (1489) bound with clasps in the "K-118" binding structure. Photo 14 (at bottom): "The Bellville Hours" bound in the "K-118" binding structure.

single pieces that pass through the board in a cantilevered manner, are inlayed and sealed to the inside of the board, and (short of breaking the metal itself) cannot be separated from the bindings by normal handling. Works in the HRHRC collections that I have bound in this manner include the *Eusebius Chronicon* from 1483 (bound without clasps) and the *Sermones de Laudibus Sanctorum* from 1489 (bound with clasps). (See photos 12 and 13.)

Subsequent models included a binding for vellum manuscripts, also with fore-edge clasps. The fore-edge clasp serves particularly well for vellum by placing pressure on the textblock, which keeps the pages flat and helps insulate the textblock from the effects of changes in humidity. This model had the added feature of a sheet of hard, smooth, Japanese paper between each leaf as a possible answer to the problem of severely convoluted manuscript leaves abrading the paint pigment and gold leaf with the turning of the pages. This experimental model was sewn on a continuous Japanese paper "concertina guard," which allows the back of the sewn sections to be isolated from any adhesive used in the binding. (See photo 22.) Such a binding is referred to as nonadhesive or semiadhesive. Some of the items from the HRHRC's "Pre-1700" manuscript collection, to which the "K-118" model was applied for purposes of restoration and rebinding, were the "Texas Hours 2," "The Bellville Hours," and a two-volume "Chronique" by Jean Froissart. (See photo 14.)

Another area in which the "K-118" structure proved useful was in the restoration or rebinding of photographic albums. Occasionally the intent of an artist will dictate that his or her photographs remain in "bound format" to retain their original purpose and integrity. In applying the "K-118" structure, I kept in mind two aspects of the photographic album: first, the binding structure and its relation to the pages, and second, the page that supports and displays the photographs. While the restored or rebound photographic album would be a version of the "K-118," it would incorporate the features of the "hollow-backed" rather than those of the "tight-back" structure of the previous "K-118" models. The "hollow-backed" structure allows the text to "throw-up" independently of the spine leather or cloth, that is, to "flex-up," away from the spine. (See photo 15.) This is especially beneficial when the pages are stiff and brittle, or will not "drape." The spine of the "tight-backed" structure is directly attached to the textblock and will generally result in less "throw-up" than the "hollow-backed."

In this version of the "K-118," photographs are supported by a larger piece of paper with cuts made to produce small flaps that hold the edges of the print without any kind of adhesive attachment. The photograph virtually floats in the middle of the support paper by the gentle friction from contact with the paper flaps. (See photo 16 and diagram 6.) When images are large or on thin material, they may be sandwiched between two pieces of clear polyester film to provide more planar strength when supported by the flaps. The "album page" created for the photographic images is actually a mat constructed like an envelope with a flap that tucks into the top and with a mat window cut for viewing each photograph. This combination of support and photograph can then be slid in and out of the mat-envelope in order to view the entire image area or to have access to information that may be on the back of the

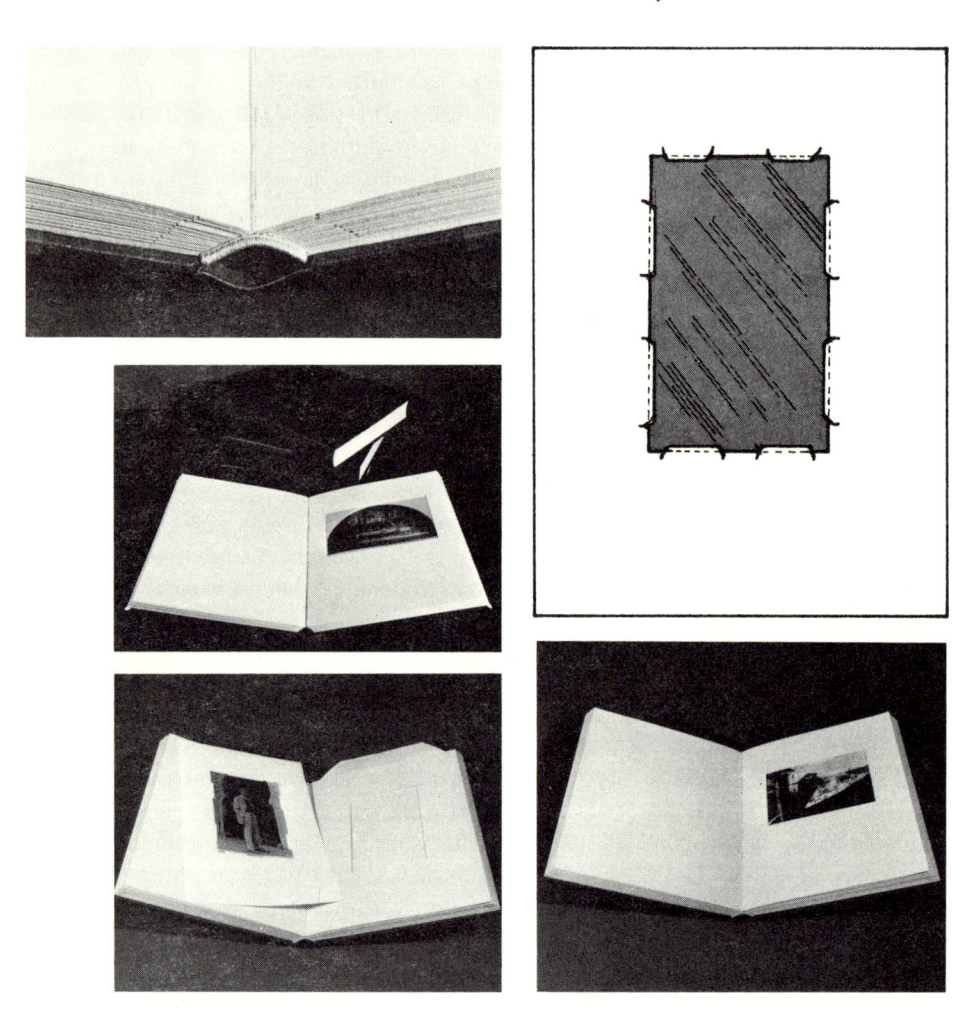

Photo 15 (top left): Illustration of the "throw-up" allowed by the use of a "hollow-back" structure for the "K-118" binding. Photo 16 (middle left): "Floating" of a photograph in its support paper by means of small flaps. Diagram 6 (top right): Illustration of structure of flaps cut to "float" the photograph in its support paper. Photo 17 (bottom left): Photograph of Paul Bowles and the "album page" structure for viewing an image through a mat window or for removing it to view the entire image area. Photo 18 (bottom right): Print of the world's first photograph in a "K-118" photographic album.

photograph. (See photo 17.) Each of these mat-pages becomes part of the album block and is then sewn into the "K-118" structure. Material for the paper support and mat-page can be chosen on the basis of the requirements of the photographic process involved. In one case, a process may require a paper or card stock with a small degree of inherent alkalinity (called alkaline-reserve) to minimize the possibility of acid migration to the photograph. Other photographic processes, however, may not tolerate this alkalinity, so that one is free to choose a support material which will provide the optimum protection necessary for a particular photographic process.

The first item in the HRHRC's Photography Collection to be rebound using the "K-118" album structure was a group of unmounted nineteenth-century "Photographs of Italy, Spain, France, Malta and Art Reproductions," all of which had been laid into a blank album. In utilizing the "K-118" structure, these photographs were mounted on support pages in four volumes of a "new" album that replaced the blank one, with the latter retained in the collection for its historical association. Another application of the "K-118" structure involved the restoration of the Center's rare copy of the beautiful 1886 publication of Peter Henry Emerson's *Life and Landscape of the Norfolk Broads*. This task was performed without apparent change in the album's format by slightly beveling the outside spine edge of the old board and by introducing the "K-118" split-tab spine lining. (See photos 19 and 20.)

The "K-118" structure also has been used to restore a Victorian publisher's cloth binding. This type of book was frequently printed on a stiff card stock, which, because of mass manufacturing methods, quickly became acidic and brittle. The requirements for this book were that the binding should retain its original format, while at the same time allowing for the use of the text by patrons. Since the original boards had a bevel all the way around the edges, this made it possible to incorporate the spine edge bevel for the "K-118" structure without altering the boards. As a result of this "K-118" structure, the inner surface of the board was flat, so that one could open the pages from first to last without their needing to flex, which is critical in the case of stiff, brittle pages. (See photo 21.)

Another viable application for the "K-118" structure is in the area of modern fine bindings. In design binding, the more options one has available, the freer one is to explore the creative aspect of the craft. The "K-118" structure offers the option of extreme flexibility of the textblock where, because of the way a page is printed, it would be necessary to have the opening expose the page down to the spine fold, as with double-page spreads for illustrations or with type that runs into the inner margin of the page.

The varied applications made possible by the "K-118" structure provide conservator, curator, and scholar alike with an additional option for the preservation of both text and binding. The fact that the "K-118" can be incorporated into virtually any other binding structure allows conservators to

Photos 19 (top left) and 20 (middle left): Two views of *The Norfolk Broads* restored in a "K-118" binding. Photo 21 (top right): *A Welcome to Alexandria* in a "K-118" photographic album. Photo 22 (bottom): An experimental model based on the "K-118" binding, showing a continuous Japanese paper "concertina guard."

produce a number of hybrids designed to solve common or unique book conservation problems. As a structure for the restored vellum manuscript, the "K-118" eliminates the necessity for the book to undergo the increased stress of a "shoulder." With the addition of clasps, the leaves can remain under pressure and somewhat isolated from the ill effects of changes in humidity. The "K-118" also can serve well as a binding for reference books that are used frequently, exploiting the remarkable strength and flexibility that are inherent to its superstructure. Finally, this style of binding is limited only by the binder's creativity and sensitivity, for it is equally suitable as a strong and heavy structure for large books, albums, or manuscripts and as a covering for the delicate and refined work of a modern fine binding or for a small Book of Hours.

As a conservator and binder, I find that the application of the "K-118" structure has proved for me an emotional adventure. Stepping into an experiment begun anonymously 500 years ago and being able to carry it further and in varied directions is a rare opportunity for any book conservator. It is humbling to realize that the two-volume set of *Speculum Naturale* might never have come to the HRHRC or that it might not have required the attention of a conservator, that instead of being brought to the lab for restoration it might have lain somewhere unnoticed, its binding information untapped forever. Even though this Nuremberg binder remains unknown, his work, fortuitously rediscovered, has ultimately made a significant contribution to the modern field of book conservation.

This portrait of H.P. Robinson accompanies an article entitled "Henry Peach Robinson," which appeared in *The Photographic Times* 17, no. 307 (5 August 1887). Presented to the Gernsheim Collection in August 1950 by Mrs. Abbott, the photographer's daughter, the portrait is mounted on a piece of backing along with and between pages 391 and 392.

Henry Peach Robinson's "Bringing Home the May": Conservation Treatment of a Nineteenth-Century Albumen Print

BY BARBARA BROWN

The foundation and core of the Photography Collection at the Harry Ransom Humanities Research Center is the Gernsheim Collection, an archive of nineteenth- and twentieth-century photographic materials and related artifacts and literature. Created by Helmut Gernsheim over many years and acquired by the University of Texas in 1963, this collection includes works by significant figures in the history of photography, one example of which is Henry Peach Robinson's photograph "Bringing Home the May." According to the typed entry in Volume 3 of Gernsheim's original inventory list, H.P. Robinson's photograph "Bringing Home the May" was presented to him in August 1950 by Robinson's daughter, Mrs. Edith Abbott.[1] In his letter to Mrs. Abbott, dated 28 July 1950, Gernsheim writes that he was happy to learn from a Miss Robinson of Mrs. Abbott's offer to give him "[her] father's well-known

---

[1]Gernsheim Working Inventory List, 25 volumes, circa 1963 (unpaginated). In Vol. 3, Gernsheim's typed entry for this photograph reads: "'Bringing Home the May,' 1862. The smaller version, 19" x 8¼". Original silverprint in Robinson's original frame, from his home. Presented by his daughter, Mrs. Abbott (aged 91) in August 1950. This picture was his most ambitious composition picture, being made from 9 negatives." This last statement is a paraphrase of Robinson's comments in his article "Autobiographical Sketches, Chapter VII," in *The Practical Photographer* 9, no. 98 (February 1898): 29-34. Immediately following the typed entry, Gernsheim writes: "According to H.P.R. this was the only decent copy surviving," and then cites the preceding article. However, as noted in the inventory entry, this photograph is a smaller version (approx. 19 x 8¼ inches) as opposed to the large version (approx. 40 x 15 inches) that Robinson first made. Correspondence dated 20 August 1988, from Margaret F. Harker (see footnote 2 below) to Roy Flukinger (curator of the HRHRC's Photography Collection), indicates that this photograph was probably made from a single negative that was "copied from the combination print, as a quantity of these [smaller] prints were made [by Robinson] to distribute to members of the P[hotographic] S[ociety], as stated in the P[hotographic?] J[ournal] of 15 Sept. 1863, p. 347." See also the article cited by Gernsheim, above. That Mrs. Abbott presented the photograph (now in the HRHRC Photography Collection) to Gernsheim is corroborated by correspondence between Gernsheim and Mrs. Abbott which is now part of the Center's manuscript collections. The nine original negatives, as well as the larger version of the photograph, are part of the Royal Photographic Society collections.

picture 'Bringing Home the May'." Gernsheim then goes on to say that he was pleased that he would be able to show at least one of Robinson's major works in the 1951 exhibition, "Masterpieces of Victorian Photography," which he had been asked by the Arts Council to arrange at the Victoria and Albert Museum. The purpose of this exhibition was to commemorate the first international exhibition of photography, held at the Crystal Palace in 1851. In her reply, dated 31 July 1950, Mrs. Abbott invites Gernsheim to come to her home, and observes, "I am the last of my generation, and except for Margaret, none who [sic] take any interest in photography, so I am glad to place this, which I believe was my father's first composition photograph, in a permanent collection."[2] In accepting her invitation, Gernsheim gently corrects her photo-history chronology, noting that "Fading Away" (1858) was actually Robinson's first composition photograph, and that "Bringing Home the May" was done four years later.

"Bringing Home the May" is an albumen print, which was the major photographic printing medium from 1855 until around 1895. The albumen process was the discovery of French photographer Louis Désiré Blanquart Evrard, who first announced it on 27 May 1850. Albumen, the white of a hen's egg, was used to form a binder layer on the surface of the paper, and in this layer the silver image would be formed upon exposure to light. The albumen was prepared by beating salted egg white into a froth and then allowing it to settle back into liquid form. In *Care and Identification of 19th-Century Photographic Prints*, James M. Reilly describes the making of albumen paper as "a floating process in which individual sheets were carefully rested on the surface of the solution, then gently lifted off and hung vertically to dry."[3] In order to be used, the albumen-coated sheets then had to be rendered light-sensitive, which was accomplished by floating the sheets "albumen side down in a tray of 10% silver nitrate solution. . . . [T]he sensitized paper did not keep well, [thus] sensitizing, printing, and processing were usually done the same day."[4]

For a number of years, photographers coated their own papers, but in the 1850s an industry grew up in response to the increased demand for albumenized papers.[5] Finding a suitable paper base, or "raw stock," was one of

[2] Margaret is possibly the Miss Robinson to whom Gernsheim refers in his initial correspondence to Mrs. Abbott. On page 84 of Margaret F. Harker's *Henry Peach Robinson, Master of Photographic Art, 1830-1901* (New York: Basil Blackwell, Inc., 1988), the author mentions a Margaret Winwood Robinson, daughter of Ralph Winwood Robinson, granddaughter of H.P. Robinson, who managed a photography studio in Guildford, while her father, Ralph, operated the studio in Redhill which he had opened in 1901, following H.P.R.'s death. Margaret W. Robinson continued in practice at the Guildford studio until 1946.

[3] James M. Reilly, *Care and Identification of 19th-Century Photographic Prints* (Rochester: Eastman Kodak Co., 1986, Publication G-2S), p. 4.

[4] Ibid., p. 5.

[5] Ibid., p. 6.

Fig. 1: Henry Peach Robinson's "Bringing Home the May" (1862), the smaller version (19.3 x 49.6 cm.). This view shows the recto of the photograph before treatment. *HRHRC Photography Collection.*

the most problematic factors involved in the making of albumen paper. The paper base "had to be a thin, smooth sheet of exceptional purity and quality" because of the floating method used to coat and sensitize the sheet;[6] "if the paper base was too thick, it became too stiff to manipulate when floated on the sensitizing solution."[7] Exceptional purity of the paper was necessary due to the high reactivity of silver in the sensitizing solution. Impurities in the paper, such as traces of copper or iron (from the water and/or machinery used to process the paper pulp), precipitated the silver in the sensitizing solution onto these spots, causing dark, dendritic flecks in the print and corresponding "blank" specks in the image. Since the factory-made albumen paper was not light-sensitive, the photographer still had to sensitize it himself, and once it was sensitized, it had to be used almost immediately.[8] Not until the 1870s did pre-sensitized, factory-made albumen paper become available on the market.[9]

Albumen printing, like the other early photographic printing processes, was a *printing-out process*; that is,

> the image appears spontaneously during exposure to light through a negative, not needing chemical development. The print would then be washed to remove excess free silver nitrate and unexposed silver chloride, then it would generally be bathed in a gold toning solution. This step "originated in 1841 as an improvement in the daguerreotype process, and was first applied to paper prints in 1847."[10]

The toning solution, which contained gold chloride, altered the image color on silver printing-out papers from a reddish brown to purple, and it improved the stability of the silver image by converting it partly to gold.[11] The toned print would be washed in clear water for a few minutes, then the image would be "fixed"—that is, any light-sensitive substances would be removed in a solution containing "hypo" or sodium thiosulfate (called "hyposulfite of soda" in the nineteenth century), leaving an image of metallic silver. Residual thiosulfate compounds were then removed in a final water wash.

Alan Vertrees, in the 1982 publication, *Perspectives on Photography*,[12] and Margaret F. Harker, in her biography/catalogue raisonnée of Henry Peach

---

[6]Ibid.

[7]Ibid. Reilly also notes here that "during the nineteenth century, only two paper mills in the world, both located in Europe, were able consistently to produce paper good enough to use for albumenizing."

[8]Ibid., p. 7.

[9]Ibid.

[10]Ibid., p. 5.

[11]Ibid.

[12]Alan Vertrees, "The Picture Making of Henry Peach Robinson," *Perspectives on Photography*, ed. Dave Oliphant and Thomas Zigal (Austin: Humanities Research Center, 1982), pp. 78-101.

Robinson,[13] have reviewed Robinson's method(s) of composite photography. Both Vertrees and Harker refer to Robinson's description of the processes he went through in composing and making his composite photograph "Bringing Home the May," which the photographer himself had discussed in an article in the February 1898 issue of *The Practical Photographer*.[14] Robinson notes in this article that the picture derived from his reading of the "May" section of Edmund Spenser's poem the "Shepheard's Calendar." With the picture inspired in his mind "almost as plainly as if it had been already photographed," Robinson then began preliminary sketches and drawings for the composition, often combining pencil, watercolor, and cut-out figures from "test" photographs.[15] As part of this composite process, Robinson made notes regarding how much (in terms of images and elements of the composition) should go on each plate (i.e., negative), where the best places would be for the joins in the final image to appear, and marked these notes on a full-sized sketch.[16] The models, costumes, and accessories then had to be selected and prepared, and specific directions written on the sketch "so that the photographer should have as little to think of as possible when the important moment [of taking the negative] arrived."[17] Another consideration (and one which was beyond the photographer's control) was the weather: for this picture, the negatives could only be taken when "the May" was in bloom, which "does not last above a fortnight," and sunlight was necessary for photographing the figures.[18] The initial printing was difficult for at least two reasons: "The paper had to be specially made as there was none on the market of that size [i.e., 40x15 inches]" and each of the nine wet plate collodion negatives had to be printed separately. (Subsequently, Robinson "fit the negatives with registration marks," which did help somewhat to simplify the printing process.)[19]

Prior to 1972, little, if anything, was known or recorded concerning the condition of the "Bringing Home the May" in the HRHRC Photography Collection. At that time the curator of the Photography Collection, Roy Flukinger, noted the unstable physical condition of the photograph and the fact that it had been removed from its frame, which was stored beside it. The photograph, which was mounted on pulpboard, was slightly wider than the frame that had housed it. As evidenced by physical damage and by a lesser degree of yellowing and discoloration, the left and right edges of the print appeared to have been folded around the edges of the mount when it had been

---

[13]Harker, *Henry Peach Robinson, Master of Photographic Art, 1830-1901*.

[14]Robinson, *The Practical Photographer*, p. 30.

[15]Ibid. Unfortunately for researchers and historians today, Robinson notes a few lines down in the article that he had "recently destroyed a quantity of [the] preliminary drawings" for this picture.

[16]Ibid.
[17]Ibid.
[18]Ibid.
[19]Ibid.

fitted into the frame. Subsequently, the mounted photograph had been installed in a window mat of museum board using white cloth tape as hinges. It was in this condition, housed in the museum board window mat, that the photograph arrived in the Conservation Lab in 1987.

Attached to the verso of the back matboard, with masking tape along three sides, was a folder of polyester film containing a label written by Gernsheim, which appears to be one that he had attached to the verso of the framed format of the photograph. (The inscription is similar to the typed inventory entry mentioned earlier.)[20] Two pieces of matboard were attached to the mount of the photograph with pieces of white cloth tape on the recto, at the top and bottom edges (see fig. 1). The two edge portions of the photograph were not attached to these pieces of matboard, except for the top right edge verso of the fragment (upper right), which was attached to a piece of the white cloth tape. The mount was deteriorated and acidic (as noted in tests discussed below). Visible along the top and bottom edges of the mount, which extended slightly beyond the edges of the photograph (approximately ⅛ inch at most), were six vertical graphite marks—three each across the top and bottom—whose meaning was unclear. No other marks were visible on the mount, recto or verso. Thus, it was decided in conjunction with the curator that this topmost layer of the mount would, as much as possible, be retained intact, so that efforts could perhaps be made to determine if the graphite marks extended behind the photograph and whether or not they had any significance.

The primary support of the albumen print (the paper support or base of the photograph) was considerably creased, cockled, and cracked along the left and right sides, and exhibited these problems to a lesser degree overall. The right side portion of the photograph had split horizontally in two, and the top half was completely detached from the rest of the object. (This piece was barely held in place by a stray corner of the white cloth tape at the edge of the mount.) There were two tiny areas of loss adjacent to the cracks on the right side, and several areas along the bottom edge of the photograph were detached from the mount.

The albumen binder layer (or coating) was, and still is, considerably yellowed as a result of the natural aging of the protein. This deterioration, which had been accelerated by prolonged exposure to light and/or to conditions of high relative humidity, can be slowed, but is not reversible. There is an overall crazing (i.e., a very fine crackle pattern) exhibited by the binder, which results from the differential expansions of the binder and paper support in the presence of moisture. There are slight scratches and abrasions overall, some with corresponding loss in the binder layer—most noticeably in

[20]The inscription, written in blue ink, reads: "'Bringing Home the May' in original frame. Composition photograph by H.P. Robinson, (1861) [*sic*] who called it his most ambitious effort since it was done from 9 negatives. Presented to me by his daughter, Mrs. Abbott, in August 1950."

the upper right, approximately 1½ inches from the top edge. Prior to treatment, a small pink accretion was visible on the cheek of the second figure from the left, and there was a layer of surface grime overall.

The photolytic (printed-out) silver image has an overall brownish tonality, and has lost detail in the highlight areas, as well as in some deeper shadows. This is due partly to the deterioration of the silver image material (affected/accelerated by the conditions noted for the binder, above), and partly to the deterioration of the binder, with losses in the image corresponding to the damaged areas in the binder and support.

Under low magnification with the stereomicroscope, tests on fiber samples taken from the mountboard were carried out using solutions which, by changing color, indicate the presence of acidity and of groundwood/lignin.[21] The test for acidity registered positive (the Chlorophenol Red solution went from a purplish color to yellow as the fibers became stained), as did the test for the presence of groundwood/lignin (the Phloroglucinol solution went from yellow to a magenta color as it was absorbed by the fibers). The positive results of both of these tests indicated that the mount contained groundwood/lignified components and was acidic—physical and chemical characteristics which are detrimental to photographic materials.

Spot tests for solubility were also carried out, under the stereomicroscope, in inconspicuous areas of the artifact, near the edge(s). These tests indicated that the support, binder, and image components were not soluble in, nor apparently adversely affected by, either water or ethanol (although the adhesive between the photograph and the backing did appear to be water-soluble), or by a 1 to 1 mixture of the two solvents. These solvents, or combinations thereof, were tested as options to consider in case the backing/mount could only be safely removed from the photograph (in as intact a state as possible) by immersing the entire object. Although backing removal is not necessarily a simple treatment or one to be considered lightly, in this particular case it was determined to be necessary for the preservation of the object. The poor-quality mountboard was brittle, deteriorated, and did not adequately or safely support the entire photograph, as evidenced by the unattached, damaged edges of the albumen print. Also, if the mounted photograph were picked up or lifted along an edge or corner, a piece of the mountboard could snap off, tearing or otherwise damaging the photograph.

The fragile, unstable physical condition of the mounted albumen print, and the damages it had already sustained, placed the object on the curator's priority list for conservation treatment. In its (then) current condition, the photograph could not be safely handled for viewing or study, much less exhibited. After careful examination of the object using the stereomicroscope

[21] Lignin is a component of wood and ground-wood pulp paper which degrades to produce acidic decomposition products and peroxides, thus contributing to the deterioration of paper and photographic materials.

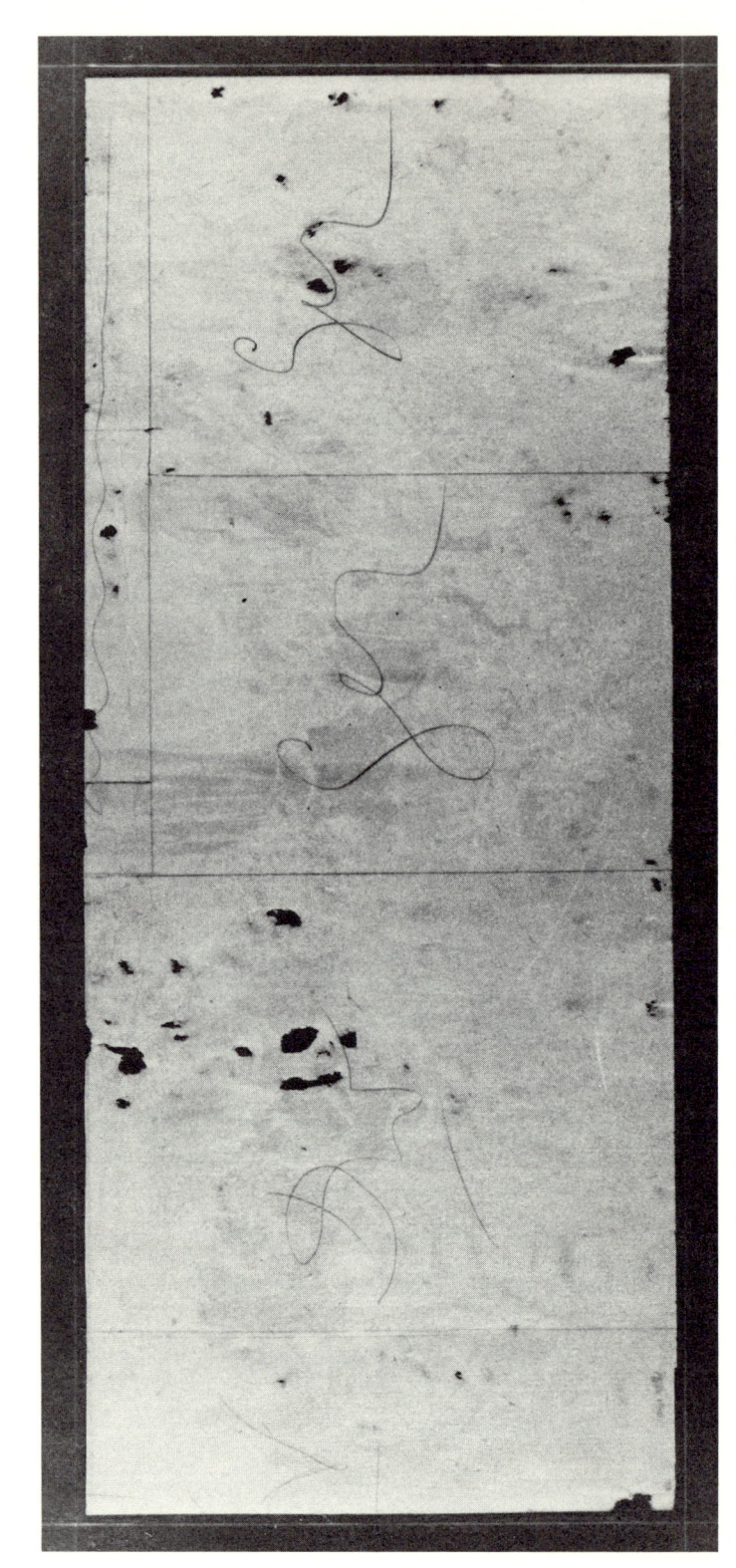

Fig. 2: Backing sheet of H.P. Robinson's "Bringing Home the May," after treatment. Note the faint negative image of the photograph that appears on the backing sheet, as well as the lines and marks in graphite.

as well as the unaided eye and the testing discussed above, a conservation treatment was proposed to preserve the photograph and to make it more accessible for safe viewing and study. The treatment proposal was first written up and discussed with the curator of the Photography Collection before being carried out with his approval.

The matboard secondary supports were detached from the central mountboard by cutting the white cloth tape along the butt-join between the boards and the mount. Then, the outermost backing layers of the pulpboard mount were split away, using a Teflon® spatula. This was done by working from the verso of the object, with the recto face down against acid-free neutral glassine (on a blotter to cushion and protect the photograph). Remaining backing material was also mechanically reduced, by using the Teflon® spatula and microspatulas. As the layers became thinner, scalpels and a sanding block were used until there only remained the final facing layer(s) of the mount, which was adhered to the verso of the albumen print. Because the photograph was adhered overall to the mount, it could not be split away safely or easily from the mount, or, conversely, the mount from it—not, that is, if the facing sheet of the mount, directly behind the photograph, were to be retained intact. Also, because the mount was of dense board, water would not easily pass through it. Thus, the mechanical thinning and/or reduction of the mountboard was carried out to reduce the amount of time the object might need to be immersed.

The white cloth tape was removed from the upper right fragment of the photograph by using a methyl cellulose poultice, followed by use of a microspatula to lift the attachment and poultice away from the surface of the object. Surface grime on the photograph (including the fragment) was removed by first carefully brushing the surface with a soft bristle brush. This was followed by gently rolling small, slightly moistened swabs over the surface of the albumen print. The stereomicroscope was used to magnify the small pink accretion and the area of the photograph's surface on which it was located. This magnification improved visibility while working on the photograph and thus helped protect it from being treated beyond the area of the accretion, which was removed by a moistened swab, followed by the use of a small bamboo probe.

The albumen print was misted recto and verso with distilled water to dampen/humidify it evenly, and was then immersed, recto up—on a support of thin polyester webbing laid over fiberglass screening and rigid polypropylene screening—into a bath of distilled water, to aid in the removal of the remaining backing layer and any adhesive residues on the verso of the photograph. After 30 minutes, a thin sheet of polyester film was placed over the recto of the photograph in the bath, and both the polyester film and the photograph were lifted together from the bath and placed recto down upon a light table. Using a microspatula, the remaining layer of backing paper was then lifted away from the verso of the photograph in two sections, following the join-line of the two pieces of paper composing this final backing layer, which was set aside and retained. Meanwhile, residual adhesive on the verso of the photograph was reduced/removed using small wads of cotton moistened in distilled water. The photograph was bathed, as described above, three more times, to reduce darkening/discoloration in the paper support.

Upon the removal of the backing sheet from the verso of the photograph, the recto of the backing sheet was found to exhibit several lines and calligraphic marks in graphite. The area is marked vertically into thirds, approximately, and a horizontal line extends from the left edge halfway across the sheet, approximately one inch from the bottom edge of the sheet. The significance (if any) of the marks and lines is still unclear.

As the backing sheet and the photograph dried (after the first bath), a negative (reverse tone) image of that in the photograph became visible on the verso of the photograph support and on the (recto) side of the backing sheet, which had been in contact with the photograph (see figs. 2 and 3). These "negative" images indicate deterioration, resulting from acid migration from the backing material combined with photo-oxidation. The binder and support of this photograph are quite thin, and could have allowed considerable transmission of light in the lower density (highlight) areas of the image. Photo- and chemical-oxidation reactions may have been accelerated by exposure to conditions of high temperature and relative humidity.

The photograph was removed from the final bath and placed recto down, on polyester film, on the light table. The tears, cracks, and the fragment were then aligned and mended using Japanese tissue (a lightweight, kozo [mulberry fiber] paper—in this instance, machine-made) and wheat-starch paste. While still damp/wet, the photograph was then lined using the same tissue and paste. This particular tissue is lightweight enough to be used with this albumen print, yet quite strong, owing to the long fibers of which it is composed. Also, being machine-made, this tissue has a definite grain direction (more so than handmade Japanese tissue), which was a consideration in that the albumen print's paper support also had a definite grain direction. In lining the photograph, the tissue was laid cross-grain to the grain of the photographic support in order to reduce the tendency of the albumen print to curl. (As noted earlier, the albumen binder layer and the paper layer support respond to changes in relative humidity at different rates and to varying degrees. The albumen layer contracts considerably more under drier conditions than does the paper, thus pulling the paper with it, which causes the print to curl.) Another reason for lining the photograph was to provide reinforcement to the mends and those areas of physical damage.

Due to the thin physical structure of the albumen print, and the general tendency of this particular photographic medium to curl when not mounted or similarly restrained, it was decided that the photograph, once lined, would be remounted onto a new, acid-free, neutral secondary support. A two-ply paper meeting these specifications was prepared for use as the new secondary support by stretch lining it on polyester fabric over plexiglass using an aqueous solution with 3% methyl cellulose. Next, the lined photograph was mounted onto this paper support using the same methyl cellulose solution. This assembly was then allowed to dry under tension, beneath polyester webbing, blotters, a pressing board, and weights.

Any lifting binder and/or edges along cracks and tears were set down using methyl cellulose (diluted as needed from the 3% solution). Areas of loss along cracks and tears were filled using a slurry of cellulose powder mixed with distilled water and methyl cellulose. This procedure of filling losses was carried out under the stereomicroscope, as was the next step of in-painting, or cosmetic re-integration, which was carried out using watercolor, with dilute methyl cellulose added as needed to obtain a surface gloss similar to that of the

Fig. 3: Detail of H.P. Robinson's "Bringing Home the May," during treatment. Shown here is part of the negative (reverse tone) image that appeared on the verso of the photograph with the mount and final backing layer removed.

Fig. 4: Recto of H.P. Robinson's "Bringing Home the May," after treatment.

photographic binder. This latter step was performed only on the fills in areas of loss but not carried over onto the rest of the image area.

The lined and (re-)mounted photograph was then removed from the polyester fabric/plexiglass mounting-and-drying support system, and excess mountboard was trimmed away. For additional support and protection, whether for handling during study or for exhibition, the mounted photograph was hinged into a window mat of acid-free, neutral, (6-ply) museum board, using a long-fibered, handmade, Japanese tissue and wheat-starch paste. (The photograph, after treatment, is shown in fig. 4.) The two sheets composing the remaining (original) backing layer were rejoined and mended using heat-set tissue, and the backing sheet was then encapsulated between polyester film, which was sealed using the sonic welder. (The backing sheet, after treatment, is shown in fig. 2.)

As a result of this conservation treatment, the physical structure of the photograph has been made more secure and stable, and chemical deterioration has been considerably slowed. Both the conservation care described here and the proper curatorial care and storage received in the Photography Collection will contribute to the preservation of this work by a "master of photographic art." "Bringing Home the May," which Henry Peach Robinson considered "[his] most ambitious effort, but perhaps not [his] best picture,"[22] is now more safely accessible for viewing and for study, so that current and future generations will have an opportunity to see and appreciate one of the greater technical undertakings of a major figure in the history of photography.

[22]Robinson, *The Practical Photographer*, p. 29.

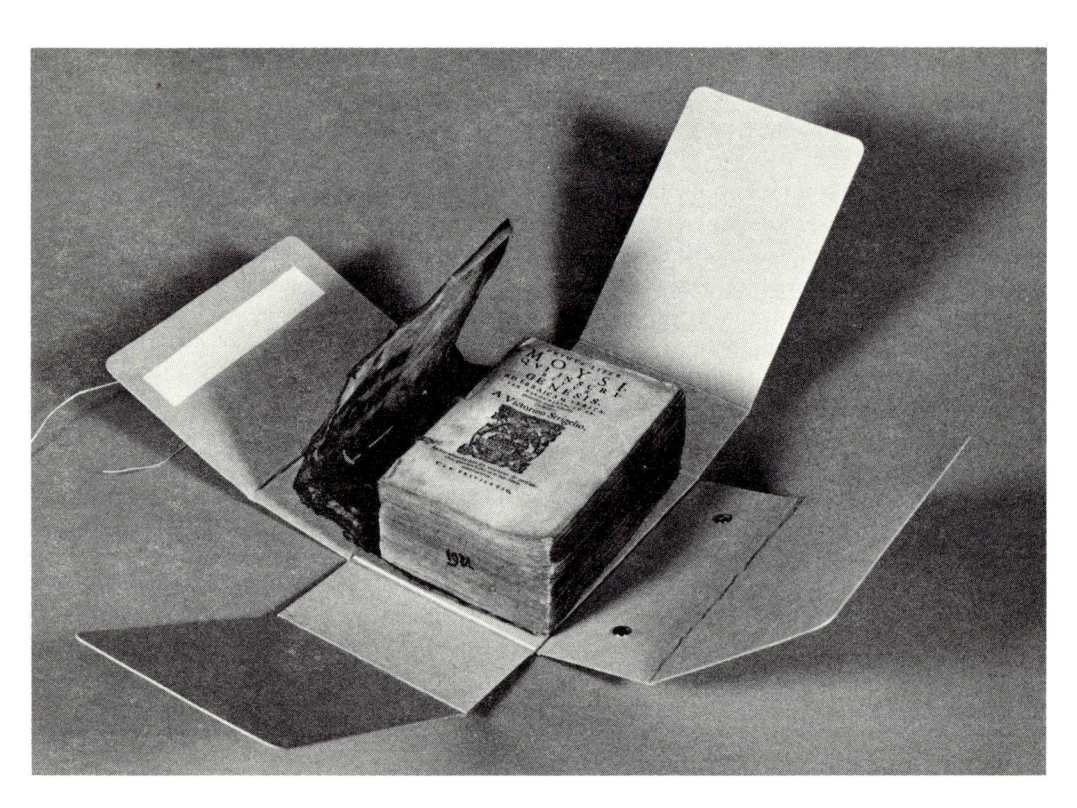

This copy of *Primvs liber Moysi, qui inscribitur Genesis . . . a Victorino Strigelio*, printed in "Lipsiae" in 1561, has been placed in a phase box because of its detached cover and loose endsheets.

Housing, When and Why

By Frank Yezer

Telephone calls to the Conservation Department of the Harry Ransom Humanities Research Center frequently go something like this: "I have an old family Bible. Can you fix it and how much does it cost?" The item may be a letter, document, or photograph, but the question is still the same. As Assistant to the Chief Conservator and supervisor of the Preservation Section, I receive a number of these calls, which I refer to our list of conservators in private practice. Some callers still ask me to tell them how much it will cost. Most people have no idea as to what is involved in the repair or treatment of an artifact and can be shocked by the price of professional services. For this reason I avoid giving telephone estimates. Not only are repairs and treatments expensive because of the time and expertise required to complete them but there may be problems not readily discernible to the untrained eye.

Institutions face a greater problem. Their collections may number in the millions: it is neither economically nor physically possible to repair every book, manuscript, or photograph that is deteriorating or damaged. An army of conservators would be needed for an effort like that. Consider also that conservation treatment may result in physical changes to original materials and structures, even when repairs are kept to a minimum. Sometimes it is best to do nothing. Before conservation is considered as an option, conservators ask questions like these: Is the artifact functional? Will it deteriorate if left in its present state? Are we going to alter its value as an historical object? To illustrate possible questions and choices facing conservators working at the HRHRC, I will use the copy of a 1561 printing of the first two books of the Old Testament, Genesis and Exodus, which I recently purchased for my own personal collection.

At first I thought this book would be a perfect candidate for conservation binding (which I would do myself, since bookbinding is an area of my own training though not part of my duties at the Center), but my examination revealed a fairly sturdy and readable textblock. In order to protect the title page from abrasion and to provide additional strength to the spine, I could add endsheets and spine reinforcements. The cover of parchment (a generic term for either parchment or vellum) had been lettered in black and red on both sides, and was probably cut from an early manuscript. Tears in the cover appeared where two alum-tawed thongs (sewing supports) had been laced in, as was the practice in the fifteenth and sixteenth centuries. Because of the lettering on both sides, the parchment cover could be difficult to repair. Perhaps it was better left alone. Still attached to the parchment cover were remnants of an endband, now mostly seen as a decorative addition to the top and bottom of a book. The remnants suggested that the endbands were made of small pieces of vellum wrapped around alum-tawed thongs, glued to the spine, and then sewn to the book with a colored thread similar in weight to that used in sewing the text. What a mistake it would be to rebind this 433-year-old book! Too bad that modern books are not made with comparable materials and care! Until I could find time to make the repairs, I would place the volume in a simple enclosure to protect it from dust and abrasion. This we call in Conservation a "housing" or being "housed."

To most people a house means a place to live which is affordable, has enough space to be comfortable, and furnishes protection from the weather. To the curator, librarian, and conservator, the meaning is much the same. A good housing structure for a book, print, manuscript, or photograph is relatively inexpensive, provides adequate space, and offers protection from the environment. It is not a dream house but it is a sturdy dwelling. A craftsman can build a housing structure that is both sturdy and beautiful—many rare objects deserve that degree of care. Institutions like the HRHRC have a great many rare items, but numbers and considerations of time require that most of these items be stored in simple but sturdy enclosures. The type of structure needed depends on the object it is meant to protect. Boxes, folders, sleeves, and binders are forms of housing that provide collection materials with protection from external damage and help maintain them in their present condition.

When the HRHRC Department of Conservation was founded in 1980, it was decided that each of the departments (Reading Room, Cataloging, Manuscripts, Iconography, Photography, and Theatre Arts) would require that some of its staff members address the immediate housing needs of that section. This meant that materials found to be in need of fast and effective housing would be handled by staff members responsible for those materials; the Conservation Department would care for the rare materials that needed more involved treatment. The program has been very productive: these "housing units" have been responsible for preserving thousands of books, documents, photographs, and manuscripts. Our year-old Preservation Section has been fortunate to have the assistance of the Cataloging Department housing unit supervised by Darnelle Vanghel. With her ideas and assistance, we have designed at least two enclosures which are a marked improvement over those previously used. One of the benefits of our collaboration is the discussion of how these enclosures should work, how practical they are, how much time is needed to make them, and what materials should be utilized.

Materials intended for housing must be made from products that do not self-destruct, products that are acid-free and lignin-free. While we do not have the capability to clear the air immediately of harmful pollutants, we do have sufficient information to help us choose products that are free of harmful acid and lignin. A statement from William Hollinger's Conservation Resources catalog gives a brief idea of what acid deterioration is: "Acids attack the bonds which hold together the glucose rings, the cellulose chains, the microfibrils, the bundles and fibers."[1] (These rings, chains, fibrils, bundles, and fibres are the fundamental structures that compose the fibrous web we know as paper.) From the same source we find these comments: "Lignin is a very large complex organic molecule which binds the cellulose together in a tree" and which "will greatly hasten a paper's demise by breaking down in myriad different ways to yield many different acids and peroxides."[2] When products are acid-free and lignin-free, they are said to be archival. Many archival materials incorporate alkaline compounds, or buffers, to reduce their susceptibility to acid attack. Placing a clean sheet of paper in an old manila envelope is like exposing a healthy child to a contagious environment. To protect the well-being of an artifact, the conservator must select from available materials those that will not expose the healthy book or manuscript to contagious ingredients or by-products.

With the proper materials at hand, there are many ways to house collection items. Simple folders offer sound protection for manuscripts, works of art on paper, photographs, and other items that can be stored flat in map drawers or vertically in document cases. A document case is a rectangular box about 15 inches long, 10 inches high, and 5 inches wide, with an attached lid. Properly housed, individual manuscript leaves are first placed in polyester sleeves, then file folders, and finally in document cases, which make the items accessible at the same time that they protect them when not in use. Groups of these cases look neat and orderly when shelved and labeled, with their contents well protected and ready for researchers on request.

Among the most useful and versatile enclosures is the phase box. In their article, "The Phase Box: A Construction Procedure," published in the HRHRC manual, *Conservation of Archival Materials* (1985), Patricia Tweedy and Craig Jensen write:

> The phase box was developed in 1971-72 at the Library of Congress to house deteriorated and otherwise damaged library materials. Conceived as a temporary housing, the phase box was designed to enclose damaged books compactly along with any or all loose parts, until proper conservation treatment could be obtained. . . . An econom-

---

[1] William K. Hollinger, *Conservation Resources, Archival Storage Materials and Conservation Supplies* (Springfield, Virginia: Conservation Resources International, Inc., 1988), p. 5.
[2] Ibid., p. 8.

ical, easily constructed, and conservationally sound housing, the phase box has been used successfully by many institutions, often as a permanent housing and for items other than books.[3]

The phase box option is particularly attractive when there are innumerable shelves of books that need care and that cannot expect the treatment that is reserved for the rarest or most frequently used items. Lost pages, abraded leather, and loose covers are problems that the phase box will not cure but can help keep from becoming worse. Made from two archival quality boards laminated together, it is a simple and effective design. This and the tuxedo case (for thinner books and pamphlets) are enclosures that can be produced in 20 to 30 minutes with a minimum of equipment. Although it is possible to make a phase box with ruler, knife, and a few other simple tools, it is effort-saving and time-saving to have a board cutter and board creaser available. Both structures are made from acid-free and lignin-free board, .040 inch or .060 inch for phase boxes and .020 inch for tuxedo cases.

Phase boxes are generally for larger and heavier volumes and require a board thickness that will ensure adequate protection for the often fragile book. Tuxedo cases, named for the formal appearance of the tie-like front lap, use thinner board, and while they do not have the stiffness of a phase box, tuxedo cases adequately protect the thinner books or pamphlets for which they were designed. Although different, each is made similarly: two pieces of the respective boards are measured to the dimensions of the book, one to enfold the length of it and the other to cover its width. After being glued together at their centers and allowed to dry, the boards of the phase box are fitted with brass rivets, while the tuxedo case relies on a simple cutout flap and slot.

Not many enclosures are more useful than the phase box. Staff members involved in preservation at the HRHRC have adopted it for magazines and newspapers, and many other variations have evolved from its design. Recently James Stroud, Chief Conservation Officer, and I modified this structure by adding a walled tray to the center, making it useful for glass plate negatives, or books that need less than a rare book box but more than a phase box.

On another occasion, Darnelle Vanghel asked if I could find a product for protecting records, their paper or plastic sleeves, and their outer jackets. After fruitlessly searching catalogs, I suggested that we pool our thoughts and design one. The final structure is not complicated but it does require skill, patience, and about 20 minutes to make. An outer part consists of two pieces of cover board a little larger than the record jacket and held together by a strip of glued cloth. The inner sleeve is more complicated. Picture a piece of square

---

[3]Craig Jensen and Patricia Tweedy, "The Phase Box: A Construction Procedure," in *Conservation of Archival Materials*, Fourth Annual Seminar (Austin: Harry Ransom Humanities Research Center, 1985), p. 22.

To protect its damaged spine covering, this copy of *Old French Title Pages*, printed by the Grabhorns in 1924 and signed by Ed Grabhorn, has been housed in a tuxedo case.

paper twice the size of a record jacket, which when cut, folded, and glued will enclose the recording on three sides. When this inner sleeve is fitted into the outer sleeve, the recording is well protected by four layers of material.

A second product resulting from our collaboration was a pamphlet binder for thin music scores, playbills, and ephemera. This structure is like a book cover with an envelope inserted instead of text. None of the commercially available products met our needs, so we designed our own. By using two medium-weight lignin-free and acid-free boards connected by a strip of cloth, and an acid-free envelope glued to an inner white cloth flap, we had an inexpensive and archivally sound pamphlet binder.

With an understanding of how materials need to be protected, with basic skills in measuring, cutting, and gluing, and with certain tools to ensure accuracy and speed, library personnel can do a superb job of housing library materials. Cataloging staff at the HRHRC have for years been very skillful in making adaptations of previous structures work for materials that need special

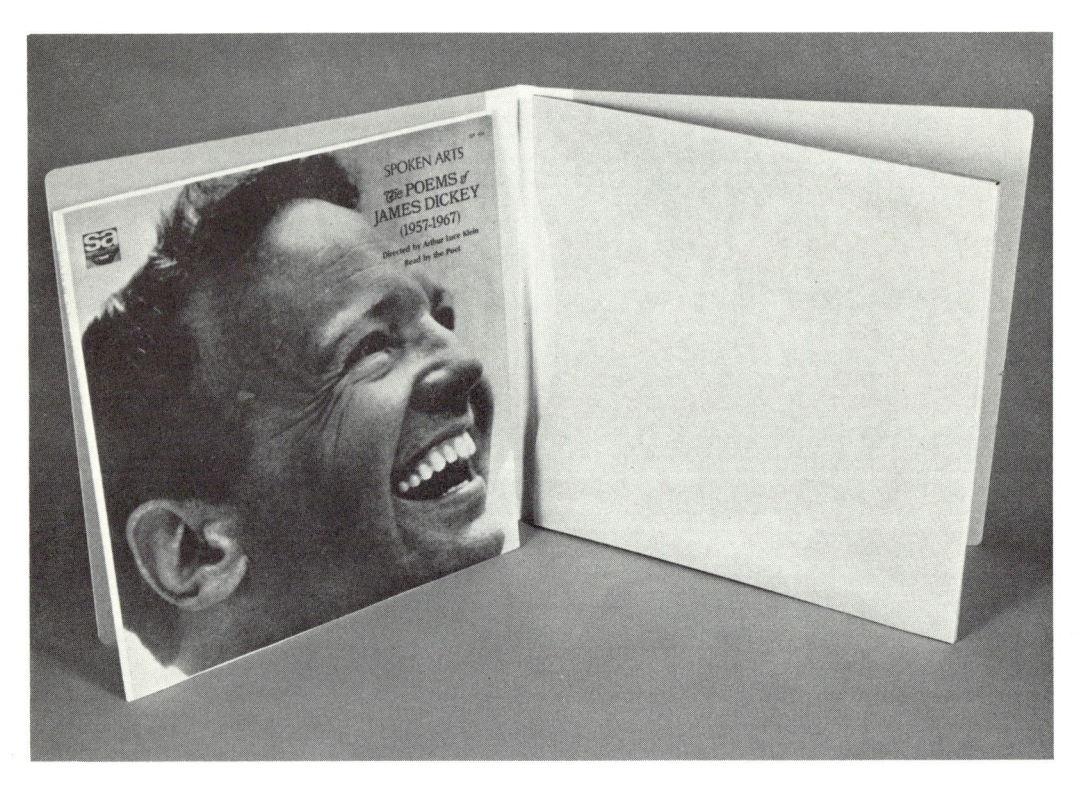

This copy of *The Poems of James Dickey (1957-1967)*, a Spoken Arts recording of the poet reading from his work, is housed in a record storage sleeve made by the Preservation Section of the HRHRC's Conservation Department.

attention. John Wright, a conservation technician, has created some ingenious systems for encapsulation of oversized posters. Volunteers of the Preservation Section have also made very helpful suggestions on alternate procedures in the manufacture of the various structures they produce. People enjoy working with their hands and are gratified when they turn out quality products.

Housing is a very important part of the preservation of collection materials at the HRHRC. With attention and perseverance a protective enclosure can be made for almost any kind of artifact. An important consideration for large collections is that the structure must be soundly designed and economical to produce. In the case of the structures discussed here, the cost of the materials and the time required for production are a fraction of those expended on involved treatments of artifacts in need of immediate attention. I like to think of housing as environmental protection rather than environmental cleanup. Housing cannot solve the problems caused by degrading paper, book leaves or prints mended with scotch tape, art works and photographs mounted on decaying boards, manuscripts written on brittle and yellowing paper, or books with spines that crack when opened, but housing is a safekeeping process, a way to make our collections safe from further external harm.

General Libraries' Conservator Patricia Tweedy and Preservation Officer Ellen Cunningham-Kruppa present a pilot preservation orientation session to professional and classified staff.

WASHINGTONIANA

The General Libraries Preservation Program: A Preliminary Report

BY ELLEN CUNNINGHAM-KRUPPA

The General Libraries of The University of Texas at Austin is a system composed of one main research library (Perry-Castañeda), an undergraduate library, eight branch libraries (Architecture and Planning, Chemistry, Classics, Engineering, Fine Arts, Geology, Life Science, and Physics-Math-Astronomy), five special collections (Asian Collection, Eugene C. Barker Texas History Center, Nettie Lee Benson Latin American Collection, Middle East Collection, and Wasserman Public Affairs Library), a storage facility (Collections Deposit Library) for low use materials, and Balcones Library, a service center on a remote campus. The Benson Collection encompasses important collections from the Río de la Plata, Chile, Peru, and Central America, in addition to significant holdings on all other countries in Latin America. The Barker Center houses not only the most comprehensive collection of Texas materials in existence but also outstanding collections on Southern United States history, the American Southwest, and the Rocky Mountain West. In 1987-88 the General Libraries' circulation of charged materials totaled over 1.8 million items. As is the case for most large research libraries, the vast numbers and types of holdings in the University's General Libraries, combined with the continual heavy use of the collections, present a daunting preservation scenario.

The General Libraries preservation program began in 1980 when the Preservation Committee (a standing committee of some years' duration) conducted a massive survey to identify preservation needs and priorities. The 147-page *Report* (1981) resulting from the survey concluded with over sixty recommendations ranked according to priority. Among the highest priorities were the appointment of a preservation officer, an increase in staff for the book repair unit, environmental improvements, and the implementation of programs for staff training and user education. While internally the Library began to focus on meeting these and other very specific preservation goals, externally it was involved in ongoing national dialogues relating to the preservation needs of major academic libraries through the participation of its director, Harold Billings, in a variety of planning and policy-making groups.

From 1983 to 1985, the director served on the Advisory Committee to the Preservation Microfilming Program of the ACRL Microform Project, and from 1983 to 1987 he served as a member of the Association of Research Libraries Committee on Preservation of Library Materials. The director also served on the Council on Library Resources Preservation and Access Committee from 1984 to 1986, and during 1986-87 he was on the National Advisory Council on Preservation as representative for the Research Libraries Advisory Committee to OCLC. In 1983 and 1986, Mr. Billings participated in the national conferences on preservation held at Wye Plantation in Wye, Maryland, sponsored by the Council on Library Resources, the Association of American Universities, and the American Council of Learned Societies. Thus, while the General Libraries preservation program grew out of the 1981 recommendations by its own in-house Preservation Committee, the program developed within a larger concurrent framework of national preservation issues and priorities.

Progress came quickly on most of the major goals established by the Committee, as staffing for the book repair unit was increased, repair materials were scrutinized as to their suitability for collections maintenance repair procedures, and a program of staff and user education was broadly designed for phased implementation. A half-time preservation coordinator was appointed and subsequent Preservation Committees continued to make gradual and steady progress toward the realization of other recommendations. An environmental monitoring program, which was instituted by library staff, identified areas of excessive humidity and temperature in the Collections Deposit Library, and measures were then adopted to remedy these environmental hazards. Meanwhile, the Preservation Committee prepared a *Disaster Preparedness Plan* and *Manual*. In the Fine Arts Library, special slotted shelving was installed for storage of phonograph recordings. Three work stations, designed by conservation consultant Sally Buchanan, were built to order for the book repair unit and major pieces of preservation equipment were acquired for use by the preservation staff. Concentrating on specific internal preservation needs, the General Libraries requested and received from 1979 to 1982 over $400,000 in federal funding from two U.S. Department of Education Title II-C grants, a Title IX grant, and a National Endowment for the Humanities grant. This funding went specifically to support preservation activities relating to research materials in the Nettie Lee Benson Latin American Collection.

In September 1988, as a graduate of the Columbia University School of Library Service Conservation Education Programs, I was named preservation officer, a full-time position which reports to the Library's assistant director and deputy assistant director for collection development. The appointment of a preservation officer signaled a broader, more active program for the General Libraries. Within the framework of overall responsibility for the planning, coordination, and management of the preservation program, I am currently concentrating on two major tasks: first, to ensure that all facets of binding and book repair operations function efficiently and are in conformity with accepted preservation standards and practices; and second, to create a five-year plan growing out of updated recommendations from the 1981 report.

An early step toward accomplishing binding and book repair goals has included a reorganization that places book repair, contract bindery preparation, and in-house pamphlet binding units under the direct supervision of the preservation officer. At present, there are eleven members of the preservation staff employed to accomplish the work of these units. The duties of the book repair unit include all repair work, ranging from very minor treatments such as page tip-ins and page mends to such major repairs as spine rebacking and resewing of textblocks. Book repair staff are also responsible for choosing the binding method to be applied to each book sent out for commercial library rebinding: recasing, double-fan adhesive binding, oversewing, or sewing through signature folds. Staff in the contract bindery preparation unit receive

Jen-Ling Ju, of the Pamphlet Binding unit, sews two boards onto a monograph to form a lace-on binding structure.

and prepare periodicals and monographs to be sent for commercial library binding. The pamphlet binding unit handles normal in-house binding of materials in pamphlet or sheet music format.

In selecting the appropriate binding methods for book repair, research libraries are faced with the fact that publishers are producing materials with narrow margins, often less than ¾ths of an inch wide. Preservation staff is now reevaluating library binding methods previously used for monographs, for such materials are many times not being read in their covers but are being photocopied, a process that places additional stress on bindings, particularly when margins are narrow and library patrons press down on spines in copying facing pages. Prior to the eighth edition of the Library Binding Institute's *Standard for Library Binding* (1986), the preferred binding method was oversewing. The eighth edition now reflects recognition of library binding as a significant preservation option that depends on the binder's (and the preservation department's) ability to take into account the physical characteristics of each volume when choosing a method that will promote its strength and flexibility. Thus, commercial library binding options once reserved for exceptional volumes, such as double-fan adhesive binding and sewing through signature folds, are now acknowledged in the *Standard* as routine binding practices. At the same time that these methods avoid the reduction of already narrow margins, they also create a strong and flexible, openable structure.

As plans develop for an efficient, full-scale repair operation that concentrates on maintenance of the General Libraries' circulating collections, I will be relying heavily on advice from newly hired conservator Patricia Tweedy, formerly with the Jensen Bindery, Conservation Services, and the Conservation Department of The University of Texas at Austin's Harry Ransom Humanities Research Center. Ms. Tweedy and her staff have initiated the planning process by reevaluating previous repair procedures, reorganizing space in the central repair unit for work efficiency, ordering appropriate materials and tools, visiting and training staff in branch libraries and special collections who perform minor book repair, and surveying these same repair units for needed tools and materials. Ms. Tweedy and I will also be working with library subject bibliographers to reaffirm their central role in collections maintenance. Presently, in the Perry Castañeda Library, a bibliographer reviews all books identified by Circulation Department staff as being in need of repair or rebinding. The reviewer determines which books should not be candidates for routine repair or rebinding procedures because of their artifactual value or state of deterioration. These books are then routed to individual subject bibliographers and are examined for appropriate preservation options. The identification of brittle books whose text is vulnerable to breakage and loss is an important component of the review process. A simple but useful test is the two-fold corner test, which is commonly administered as a quick and inexpensive method for identifying embrittlement. The corner of a page is folded forwards, then folded backwards on the same crease, and this is repeated a second time. If the paper breaks on any of these four folds it is considered to be brittle. In short, by implementing the two-fold corner test as part of the bibliographic review process, we will be able to attend to more books whose text is vulnerable to breakage and consequent loss.

Once a book's textblock has become brittle, the only way to ensure its physical longevity is through prohibitively expensive conservation treatment. For items considered important mainly because of their informational content, research libraries are choosing either to replace them (with a reprint, new edition, or microfilm) or to reproduce them (on microfilm or permanent paper). Although brittle books can many times be successfully adhesive bound, such treatment can actually prove harmful to the item by implying to users that the text is in sturdy, usable condition. Normally, brittle items holding artifactual value are not reproduced and are instead treated, boxed to await future treatment, or left alone until future technologies can lower the cost of treatment. Expenses mount quickly when the decision is made to film as well as provide conservation treatment for artifacts. Furthermore, many items (especially those which are tightly bound) could be irreparably harmed in the filming process.

The task of creating a five-year plan will necessarily include not only enhancements of the General Libraries' current activities but also new initiatives and procedures. A primary objective of Library preservation planning is the initiation and continuation of a comprehensive reformatting and collections maintenance program for the internationally preeminent Nettie Lee Benson Latin American Collection, an end consonant with the larger national preservation interests. Condition surveys of Benson Collection materials will be accomplished so that appropriate preservation options (microfilming, preservation photocopying, rebinding, repair, or conservation treatment) can be executed. The preservation of Mexican history materials is high among national, University, and Library priorities, and is a first step toward the General Libraries' larger goal of a comprehensive preservation program.

"Preservation" is often defined as the set of actions taken to prevent, stop, or retard deterioration of library materials through the management of storage environments, housing materials and techniques, and handling practices, as well as through staff and user education. Replacement is a form of preservation, as is changing the format of materials in order to preserve the intellectual content. "Conservation" implies that the actions to prevent, stop, or retard deterioration are taken through treatment of the physical condition of an item. "Preservation" is often used as the broader term encompassing both preservation and conservation. The General Libraries' longer range plans will be directed toward conservation treatment for the rare and unique non-circulating materials in the Library's collections. In the meantime, careful

Arthur Edgar, of the General Libraries' Book Repair unit, inspects and sorts books from the branch libraries.

attention is being given to preservation of these collections by housing manuscript and other archival materials in appropriate protective enclosures. For example, acid-free, lignin-free enclosures buffered with calcium carbonate can serve to prevent deteriorative acids from migrating from adjacent materials and protect materials from harmful acidic gases and pollutants in the atmosphere.

To develop and refine the five-year plan, I will be consulting with many of the General Libraries' staff in order to formulate, coordinate, and implement program plans and policies in the most effective manner. In this task I will be working closely with Dr. Mary Brennan, deputy assistant director for collection development and member of the Texas State Preservation Committee. I will also maintain active working relations with the preservation programs of other campus agencies, such as the Harry Ransom Humanities Research Center, the Tarlton Law Library, the Archer M. Huntington Art Gallery, and the Texas Memorial Museum, in order to share skills, knowledge, and plans for common preservation goals. As chair of the Preservation Committee, I will collaborate with Committee members on special and long-range projects. The 1988/89 Committee is presently concentrating its efforts on developing routine staff education programs in preservation. In meeting this goal the Committee has designed a preservation orientation session to be held each semester for all new classified and professional staff. Recently "Preservation Basics," a two-page reference text with accompanying poster, was developed to inform staff on general procedures for handling, transporting, and shelving of library materials. The Committee is also working on three new modules for *Preservation of Library Materials: a Manual for Staff*, which will deal in detail with transportation of library materials, exhibition procedures, and care and handling of service microforms. Updating the *Disaster Plan* and the Disaster Action Team *Manual* is also a high priority for the Committee.

Large-scale preservation programs are continually faced with an overwhelming amount of work to accomplish, as well as a variety of complex issues and challenges that must be addressed. The University of Texas General Libraries preservation program is fortunate to receive unequivocal support from the Library's staff and administration. Because of this support, the General Libraries preservation program is moving ahead methodically and vigorously, expanding operations to encompass a wide range of critical preservation activities.

NOTES ON CONTRIBUTORS

MARY C. BAUGHMAN, an Assistant Book Conservator at the HRHRC, received a B.A. in History from The University of Texas at Austin. She recently studied in Switzerland with the renowned design binder Hugo Peller, through a grant awarded by The John Anson Kittredge Educational Fund and as a recipient of a Samuel H. Kress Conservation Fellowship Award. Her article entitled "Book Conservation Training, Deep in the Heart of Texas" was originally published in *The New Library Scene* (1986), was reprinted in the *Guild of Bookworkers Journal* (1987), and was translated into Japanese for *Conservation and Preservation* (Tokyo, 1987). The graphic illustrations for her article were all drawn by the author.

BARBARA BROWN, the Photographic Conservator at the HRHRC, received a B.F.A. in Art History from Virginia Commonwealth University and an M.S. in Art Conservation from the University of Delaware. During internships at the Image Permanence Institute and at the International Museum of Photography/George Eastman House, she worked with James Reilly and Grant Romer, respectively. Her conservation treatment of Henry Peach Robinson's "Bringing Home the May" is the subject of another article she has written for a forthcoming publication entitled *Topics in Photographic Conservation.*

ELLEN CUNNINGHAM-KRUPPA, formerly a member of the HRHRC's Technical Staff, is now the Preservation Officer for the General Libraries of The University of Texas at Austin. She received a B.S. in Secondary Education and an M.L.I.S. from The University, as well as a Certificate in Library and Archives Preservation Administration from Columbia University. Prior to her work at Columbia, Ms. Cunningham-Kruppa was the Project Archivist at the Peabody Institute of The Johns Hopkins University.

BRUCE LEVY, formerly the Senior Book Conservator at the HRHRC, is presently in private practice in Nevada City, California. Before coming to the HRHRC he was the proprietor of the Da Vinci Bindery, doing restoration of rare books and manuscripts for such clients as the Getty Museum and Stanford University. In addition to his background in conservation, Mr. Levy has worked as a freelance commercial photographer, having studied at the Germaine School of Photography in New York City. All illustrations for his article on the "K-118" binding were photographed or drawn by the author.

SUE MURPHY is Senior Paper Conservator at the HRHRC in charge of the Manuscripts and Art on Paper Section. She received the M.A. in Art History from The University of Texas at Austin and in 1987 completed a six-months internship at The Museum of Modern Art in San Francisco where she studied methods for the treatment of paintings on canvas.

KAREN PAVELKA is an Assistant Conservator at the HRHRC in the Manuscripts and Art on Paper Section. She received a B.A. in Studio Art from the University of Minnesota and an M.L.S. from Columbia University, as well as an Advanced Certificate in Library and Archives Conservation awarded jointly by Columbia University and New York University. In 1987 she spent two months in Spain working on a preservation field project at the Castillo de Sant Genis de Vilassar.

JAMES STROUD, the Chief Conservation Officer at the HRHRC, was trained as a paper conservator in London at the Camberwell School of Arts and Crafts. Prior to coming to the HRHRC in 1980, he worked with Jacqueline Gilliam at the Fort Worth Art Museum. Recently he has been involved in conservation treatments for the Texas Declaration of Independence and the Brudenell Magna Carta.

ELLEN WEIR, formerly an Assistant Conservator at the HRHRC in the Manuscripts and Art on Paper Section, is presently working in paper conservation at the Northeast Document Conservation Center in Andover, Massachusetts. She studied Art History at the University of New Mexico, received a B.G.S. in Anthropology from the University of New Hampshire, and has done archaeological excavation fieldwork in Portsmouth, New Hampshire.

CAROL SUE WHITEHOUSE, formerly a Conservation Intern at the HRHRC, is now an Associate Conservator at Case Western Reserve University Library in Cleveland, Ohio. She received a B.A. in English from Grinnell College and an M.S. in Library Service from Columbia University, as well as a Certificate in Library and Archives Conservation awarded jointly by Columbia University and New York University.

JILL WHITTEN, a member of the HRHRC's Conservation Technical Staff, received a B.F.A. in Studio Art from The University of Texas at Austin. In addition to her work at the HRHRC, she has assisted with the installation of exhibitions in a variety of media mounted by Laguna Gloria Art Museum, the Austin Visual Arts Association, Women and Their Work, and the Texas Fine Arts Association.

Frank Yezer is Assistant to the Chief Conservation Officer at the HRHRC and Supervisor of the Center's Preservation Section. During the summer of 1986 he served as the Center's Executive Director for its Institute of Fine Binding and Book Conservation. Prior to his coming to the HRHRC, Mr. Yezer worked as an independent bookbinder, and before that was a professional dancer with the Ballet Russe de Monte Carlo, the National Ballet of Washington, D.C., and the Metropolitan Opera Company.